S. Hrg. 113–525

DEVELOPMENTS IN UKRAINE

HEARING

BEFORE THE

COMMITTEE ON FOREIGN RELATIONS
UNITED STATES SENATE

ONE HUNDRED THIRTEENTH CONGRESS

SECOND SESSION

JUNE 5, 2014

Printed for the use of the Committee on Foreign Relations

Available via the World Wide Web: http://www.gpo.gov/fdsys/

U.S. GOVERNMENT PUBLISHING OFFICE

92–458 PDF   WASHINGTON : 2015

For sale by the Superintendent of Documents, U.S. Government Publishing Office
Internet: bookstore.gpo.gov   Phone: toll free (866) 512–1800; DC area (202) 512–1800
Fax: (202) 512–2104   Mail: Stop IDCC, Washington, DC 20402–0001

COMMITTEE ON FOREIGN RELATIONS

ROBERT MENENDEZ, New Jersey, *Chairman*

BARBARA BOXER, California
BENJAMIN L. CARDIN, Maryland
JEANNE SHAHEEN, New Hampshire
CHRISTOPHER A. COONS, Delaware
RICHARD J. DURBIN, Illinois
TOM UDALL, New Mexico
CHRISTOPHER MURPHY, Connecticut
TIM KAINE, Virginia
EDWARD J. MARKEY, Massachusetts

BOB CORKER, Tennessee
JAMES E. RISCH, Idaho
MARCO RUBIO, Florida
RON JOHNSON, Wisconsin
JEFF FLAKE, Arizona
JOHN McCAIN, Arizona
JOHN BARRASSO, Wyoming
RAND PAUL, Kentucky

DANIEL E. O'BRIEN, *Staff Director*
LESTER E. MUNSON III, *Republican Staff Director*

CONTENTS

(III)

DEVELOPMENTS IN UKRAINE

THURSDAY, JUNE 5, 2014

U.S. SENATE,
COMMITTEE ON FOREIGN RELATIONS,
Washington, DC.

The committee met, pursuant to notice, at 10 a.m., in room SD–419, Dirksen Senate Office Building, Hon. Robert Menendez (chairman of the committee) presiding.

Present: Senators Menendez, Cardin, Shaheen, Murphy, Kaine, Markey, Corker, Johnson, and Flake.

OPENING STATEMENT OF HON. ROBERT MENENDEZ, U.S. SENATOR FROM NEW JERSEY

The CHAIRMAN. Good morning. This hearing of the Senate Foreign Relations Committee will come to order.

I want to welcome our panelists and thank them for taking time to share their perspective with the committee on developments in Ukraine, which appear only slightly less ominous than they did in act one of this crisis.

Now we are in the beginning of act two, with the successful election of a President by the Ukrainian people in internationally certified elections, which is a major victory for Ukraine's struggle for freedom.

Past elections in Ukraine have exhibited stark divisions between east and west. Significantly President-elect Petro Poroshenko won districts from one end of Ukraine to the other. It seems clear that the events of the past year and Russia's violation of their sovereignty unified Ukrainians as never before.

While it is clear that President Poroshenko has a mandate, the challenges he confronts are daunting. He must rebuild the Ukrainian Government and an economy which has been weakened by the previous Presidents' corruption, while countering Putin in the east.

We are committed as a nation to working with the new government and the people of Ukraine to consolidate Ukraine's democracy and economy, and help Ukraine withstand the malign tactics of its neighbor to the east. President Putin continues to direct events in Ukraine, seeking to undermine the new government and to foment discord in the east with the clear goal seeking a long-term ability to control and direct Ukraine's politics and policies.

As Catherine the Great said, "I have no way to defend my borders except to extend them," a point that seems to have a renewed poignancy today.

To counter that 18th century mindset, I welcome President Obama's announcement this week of a European reassurance initiative that will increase our presence across Europe and build the capacity of our friends such as Georgia, Moldova, and Ukraine so that they can better work alongside the United States and NATO, as well as provide for their own defense.

In my view, there are three things that are crucial for Ukraine's future. First, President Poroshenko must build a Ukrainian Government that is capable, transparent, accountable, and strong enough to meet both foreign and domestic challenges.

Second, the Ukrainian Government will have to accommodate restive citizens in the east while gaining control from foreign-directed forces.

And thirdly, the Ukrainian economy must be resurrected, including decreasing energy dependency on Russia.

At the end of the day, the creation of a viable, successful Ukraine capable of preserving its sovereignty is an unfinished legacy of the cold war, and will take time. It is a necessary goal that requires the commitment and cooperation of the Congress, the executive branch and our allies, working together.

With that, let me turn to Senator Corker for his remarks.

STATEMENT OF HON. BOB CORKER, U.S. SENATOR FROM TENNESSEE

Senator CORKER. Mr. Chairman, thank you, and thanks to our expert witnesses here who will be helpful to us, I know especially the last one, who just came in well-dressed and looking sharp.

I do want to congratulate the people of Ukraine for the election that just occurred. I know that we had a lot of observers there, including I think Jane Harman, who just walked in, and many of our colleagues. Poroshenko, who many of us had the opportunity to meet over the course of time, I think is the person today.

There are tremendous issues to overcome in Ukraine, forgetting the external effect that Russia is having on the country. There are tremendous corruption issues, energy issues, democracy issues, human rights issues, all kind of issues for any leader to have difficulty undertaking, not to speak of the external issues I just mentioned. There is no question that Russia played a role in eastern Ukraine. There is no question that they continue to play a role in eastern Ukraine. Obviously, it looks like they are back and forth between trying to negotiate with this new government and create alliances there and, at the same time, continuing to destabilize the country in other ways.

So I look forward to what our witnesses have to say relative to what our policy should be going ahead. I know there was an announcement today where Cameron and our President announced the need for new sanctions in Russia. I look forward to hearing what the witnesses have to say about that. I know numbers of us have joined together pushing for that kind of thing.

But the fact is we have tremendous challenges there. I know just having come from eastern Europe, concern for security and stability in that region is paramount right now as they have seen Russia doing what it has done. So the fact is we not only have the issue of Ukraine to contend with—and again, I know you are going to enlighten us in that regard, but also the need to show tremendous strength and perseverance relative to eastern Europe in general. So a very, very important issue of great geopolitical significance.

Thank you all for being here, and I look forward to our questions.

The CHAIRMAN. Thank you, Senator Corker.

Let me introduce our panelists—the Honorable Jane Harman, director, president, and CEO of the Woodrow Wilson International Center for Scholars, and a former colleague of mine in the House. We welcome you back to the committee. We also have with us former Ambassador to Ukraine, Steven Pifer, who is now with the Brookings Institution. Our third panelist is former Assistant to the President and Deputy National Security Advisor James Jeffrey, now the Philip Solondz Distinguished Visiting Fellow at the Washington Institute. Next is Mark Green, the president of the International Republican Institute [IRI] and former Ambassador to Tanzania, and Member of the House of Representatives. Finally, someone who is no stranger to the committee, Ken Wollack, the president of the National Democratic Institute [NDI].

Let me welcome you all to the committee.

I will advise you that all of your full statements will be included in the record, without objection. We would ask you to summarize them in about 5 minutes or so. And we will proceed in the order in which I introduced you. Jane, you are first.

STATEMENT OF HON. JANE HARMAN, DIRECTOR, PRESIDENT, AND CEO, WOODROW WILSON INTERNATIONAL CENTER FOR SCHOLARS; FORMER MEMBER, U.S. HOUSE OF REPRESENTATIVES, WASHINGTON, DC

Ms. HARMAN. Thank you, Mr. Chairman, and thank you, Ranking Member Corker. Both of you are dear friends of mine and former colleagues and also friends of the Wilson Center, and I appreciate being invited.

Everyone on the lineup here is a close friend, and I was very proud to be a member of the NDI delegation in Ukraine just a week and a half ago. It is the eighth election I have observed. NDI and IRI do this brilliantly, and it matters to have them in countries and to have teams with them who can get around.

And in that connection, on the day before the election in Ukraine, my small group, headed by former Secretary of State Madeleine Albright, met all the leading candidates, including Petro Poroshenko, who impressed me as a man capable of leading his country. And it was impressive to see his enormous victory. Would a lot of Members of the Senate not like a victory of 55 to 56 percent in a crowded field, avoiding a runoff?

At any rate, let me just make some brief comments.

This is Ukraine's third chance to get it right. Ukraine got it wrong after the wall came down. Ukraine got it wrong after the Orange Revolution. A series of governments were corrupt and not competent. This is chance three, and I think it will either work or it will be three strikes and you are out. I do not think Ukraine will get a chance like this again.

Second point. The West obviously needs to help Ukraine, and President Obama announced some aid. The IMF and the EU are poised to help. But Ukraine has to help Ukraine. This is the chance for Ukrainians to take responsibility for their future, and I do think that many Ukrainians with whom we spoke get that. I think there are five things that President Poroshenko—he will be President this Saturday—needs to do.

One is go to east Ukraine and tell the folks there—he says he is going to do this—that he favors some form of decentralization that is consistent with one Ukraine and that he wants them to serve in his government. The current Acting President Turchynov was in east Ukraine the other day, and I thought that was a good move.

Second, include the Maidan crowd, the crowd that demonstrated in Maidan so bravely over 6 months, in the new government. Some of them want to serve. Some of the current government members were in the Maidan. This has to be a different movie from Egypt. The people who were brave and courageous and wanted to change their country have to be included in the government.

Third, enforce the anticorruption laws. There are some on the books. If they need to be stronger, make them stronger. Certainly it is true that Poroshenko is himself an oligarch, as are most of the folks in senior leadership positions in Ukraine, but this is his chance to show that he is going to lead his country not just pad his bank account.

Fourth, assemble an A-plus economic team from inside and outside the country so that the tough steps can be taken to qualify for IMF and EU loans.

And fifth, welcome the Ukrainian diaspora back. There are very many smart and some wealthy Ukrainians out and about who could help their country.

Then comes the tough issue—and you mentioned this, Senator Corker—what to do about the Russians and the unrest in the east part of Ukraine. I think it is time for a united voice, all the Europeans, President Obama, and others, to call on President Putin to stop most of this violence. I am assuming there are some crazies he cannot stop, but we all know that Chechens and others are crossing the Russian border in trucks with arms. And those folks have to come home. The border has to be policed. The flow of arms has to be stopped. And Putin should tell the separatists in east Ukraine to lay down their arms.

But second, we do need more sanctions. And I would say that these sanctions against the banking industry and the economic industry and the energy—the economic sector and the banking sector have to be imposed. And I know that Europe is reluctant, but Chancellor Merkel seems to be open to this. And President Obama should press big-time to have those sanctions in place if President Putin does not respond in the shortest period of time to this demand to stop the violence in east Ukraine.

Thank you.

The CHAIRMAN. Ambassador Pifer.

STATEMENT OF HON. STEVEN PIFER, SENIOR FELLOW, THE BROOKINGS INSTITUTION, FORMER AMBASSADOR TO UKRAINE, WASHINGTON, DC

Ambassador PIFER. Mr. Chairman, Senator Corker, distinguished members of the committee, thank you for the opportunity to talk to you today about the Ukraine-Russia crisis and the United States policy response.

And, Mr. Chairman, I have submitted a written statement for the record, which I will now summarize.

Ukrainians went to the polls in large numbers on May 25 in an election that met international democratic standards. Petro Poroshenko won a resounding victory.

The President-elect now faces significant challenges. He must find a way to manage eastern Ukraine, where clashes continue between separatists and government forces. He must oversee implementation of the economic reforms in Ukraine's program with the International Monetary Fund. He must address the questions of decentralization of power.

Mr. Poroshenko also faces the major challenge of dealing with Russia. Unfortunately, by all appearances, Vladimir Putin remains opposed to Kiev's desire to draw closer to the European Union. He continues the policy that Moscow has pursued since its illegal occupation of Crimea; Russia seeks to destabilize the Ukrainian Government.

There is no evidence that Moscow has used its influence with the armed separatists in Ukraine's east to urge them to deescalate the crisis. To the contrary, Russia appears to support and encourage them. Numerous reports indicate that arms, supplies, and fighters flow from Russia into Ukraine.

Russia has legitimate interests in Ukraine, to be sure. But those interests do not mean that it should resort to force, seize Ukrainian territory, or support separatism.

The U.S. policy response appears to have three vectors. First, the administration has bolstered the political legitimacy of the Government in Kiev and targeted assistance to help Ukraine reform.

One area where Washington should do more is military assistance. The Ukrainian military needs help in strengthening its defensive capabilities. Ukrainian units in the field could use basic equipment such as tents. The decision to provide body armor, night-vision goggles, and communications equipment is welcome, if overdue.

The United States should also offer counterinsurgency advice and intelligence support. It is also appropriate to consider providing light antiarmor weapons and man-portable air defense systems, particularly since the Ukrainian military, at United States and NATO request, eliminated many of its stocks of MANPADS.

The second vector of United States policy has aimed to reassure NATO allies in the Baltic and Central European regions, who are more nervous about Moscow's intentions following the seizure of Crimea. United States and NATO military forces have deployed with the objectives of reassuring allies of NATO's commitment to their defense and of underscoring that commitment to Moscow.

On Tuesday, the President proposed a $1 billion program to increase the U.S. military presence in Central Europe. Congress should approve expedited funding for that.

The third vector of U.S. policy has sought to penalize Russia with the goal of effecting a change in Moscow's course on Ukraine. Washington has ratcheted down bilateral relations. G7 leaders, the G8 less Mr. Putin, met in Brussels instead of Sochi.

The U.S. Government has worked with the European Union to impose visa and financial sanctions on selected Russian individuals and entities. The sanctions to date, although modest, appear to have an impact. Projections of Russian GDP growth in 2014 have been reduced, and Bloomberg reports that no Russian company has been able to sell foreign currency bonds since March.

Sanctions, however, thus far have failed in their primary political purpose. Russia has not significantly altered its course on Ukraine. More robust sanctions are justified and should be applied. These could include: expanding the list of Russians targeted for visa and financial sanctions; applying targeted sanctions on the financial sector of Russia, beginning with the sanctioning of at least one major Russian financial institution as opposed to smaller pocket banks; and blocking Western companies from new investments to develop oil and gas fields in Russia.

In considering sanctions, Washington should be smart. Where possible, it makes sense to use a scalpel rather than a sledge-hammer. The U.S. Government should avoid measures that are counterproductive.

Washington should also encourage Kiev to pull together a package for a settlement of the country's internal divisions. These could provide a basis for stabilizing Ukraine. The big question, however, is whether the Kremlin would be prepared to support any settlement.

Mr. Chairman, Senator Corker, members of the committee, the Ukrainian crisis will likely continue for some time. The challenges facing Kiev are steep. Stabilization will not prove easy.

But we should remember that Ukraine has rich economic potential and a talented people. Many Ukrainians seem to recognize that they have a precious second chance to turn their country around, after the missed opportunity of the Orange Revolution.

United States policy should aim to maximize the prospects that this time Ukraine will succeed. This will be important for the people of Ukraine and for a more stable and secure Europe. Also, the best rebuke to Moscow's policy would be to see Ukraine in several years' time looking more and more like Poland: a normal, democratic, rule of law, and increasingly prosperous European state.

Thank you for your attention.

[The prepared statement of Ambassador Pifer follows:]

PREPARED STATEMENT OF AMBASSADOR STEVEN PIFER

INTRODUCTION

Mr. Chairman, Senator Corker, distinguished members of the committee, thank you for the opportunity to appear today to testify on the Ukraine-Russia crisis and how the United States should respond.

As Ukraine struggles through the ongoing crisis, Ukrainians went to the polls in large numbers on May 25 in an election that observers agreed met international democratic standards. Petro Poroshenko will take office on June 7 with renewed democratic legitimacy, having won a clear mandate from the Ukrainian electorate.

The President-elect faces significant challenges. He must find a way to manage eastern Ukraine, where clashes continue between armed separatists and government forces. He must oversee implementation of the economic reforms to which Ukraine agreed in its program with the International Monetary Fund. He must address the important questions of decentralization of power and political reform.

Mr. Poroshenko also faces the major challenge of dealing with Russia. Although Vladimir Putin said that Russia would respect the will of the Ukrainian electorate, Russian actions suggest a different approach. There is no evidence that Moscow has used its considerable influence with the armed separatists in Donetsk and Luhansk oblasts (provinces) to urge them to de-escalate the crisis. Numerous reports indicate that arms, supplies and fighters cross from Russia into Ukraine, something that Russian border guards could interdict.

What apparently triggered Russian efforts to destabilize the interim Ukrainian Government after former President Victor Yanukovych fled in February was the interim government's affirmation of its desire to draw closer to the European Union and sign the Ukraine-EU association agreement. Mr. Putin opposes that. Given that Mr. Poroshenko also supports the association agreement, Russia will likely continue its destabilization efforts.

The U.S. Government's response has been organized along three vectors: (1) bolster the Ukrainian Government; (2) reassure NATO allies unnerved by Moscow's aggressive behavior; and (3) penalize Russia with the objective of promoting a change in Russian policy. The administration generally deserves high marks on the first two vectors. More should be done, however, to raise the consequences for Moscow should it not alter its policy course regarding Ukraine.

WHY SHOULD THE UNITED STATES CARE ABOUT UKRAINE?

At a time when the U.S. foreign policy in-box is overflowing, why should Americans care about Ukraine? Let me offer three reasons.

First, Ukraine has been a good international partner of the United States for more than two decades. When the Soviet Union collapsed in 1991, Ukraine had on its territory the world's third-largest nuclear arsenal—including some 1,900 strategic nuclear warheads arming 176 intercontinental ballistic missiles (ICBMs) and 45 strategic bombers—all designed to strike the United States. Ukraine agreed to give up that arsenal, transferring the nuclear warheads to Russia for elimination and destroying the ICBMs and bombers.

In 1998, Ukraine was participating in the construction of the nuclear power plant at Bushehr in Iran. At U.S. behest, the Ukrainian Government aligned its nonproliferation policy with U.S. policy and withdrew from the project, forcing Russia to find another and more expensive provider of turbine generators for the Iranian reactor.

In 2003, following the downfall of Saddam Hussein, Kiev responded positively to the U.S. request for contributions to the coalition force in Iraq. At one point, the Ukrainian Army had nearly 2,000 troops, the fourth-largest military contingent, in country.

And in 2012, Ukraine transferred out the last of its highly enriched uranium as part of the U.S.-led international effort to consolidate stocks of nuclear weapons—usable highly enriched uranium and plutonium.

This kind of partnership merits U.S. support when Ukraine faces a crisis.

Second, as part of the agreement by which Ukraine gave up its nuclear weapons, the United States, Britain, and Russia committed in the 1994 Budapest Memorandum on Security Assurances to respect the sovereignty and territorial integrity of Ukraine and not to use, or threaten to use, force against Ukraine. Russia's illegal seizure and annexation of Crimea constitute a gross violation of its commitments under that document, as does Russia's ongoing support for separatists in eastern Ukraine. The United States and Britain should meet their commitments by supporting Ukraine and pressuring Russia to halt actions that violate the memorandum.

Third, Russia's actions constitute a fundamental challenge to the post-war order in Europe. The illegal seizure of Crimea is the most blatant land-grab that Europe has seen since 1945. The United States and Europe need to respond adequately and ensure that Russia faces consequences for this kind of behavior. Otherwise, the danger is that Mr. Putin may pursue other actions that would further threaten European security and stability.

THE SITUATION IN UKRAINE: THE MAY 25 PRESIDENTIAL ELECTION

Ukrainians went to the polls on May 25 to elect a new President. The success of that election has important implications. Since Mr. Yanukovych fled Kiev (and Ukraine) at the end of February, many Ukrainians, particularly in the east, had seen the acting government as illegitimate. The May 25 election will put in office a President with renewed democratic legitimacy.

By all accounts, the election proceeded normally in most of the country. Sixty percent of the electorate voted, an impressive number given that armed separatists in Donetsk and Luhansk—where about 14 percent of Ukraine's voters reside—prevented voting in most precincts in those oblasts.

On May 26, the Organization for Security and Cooperation in Europe election-monitoring mission released its preliminary assessment of the vote. While noting some problems, it concluded that the election was "largely in line with international commitments . . . in the vast majority of the country." Virtually all election observers—including the European Network of Election Monitoring Organizations and Committee of Voters of Ukraine—concurred in the positive assessment of the election's conduct.

According to Ukraine's Central Electoral Commission, Mr. Poroshenko won with 54.7 percent of the vote, a figure that tracked closely with the number reported in the two major exit polls released on the evening of May 25. The strength of that victory was remarkable and, by crossing the 50 percent threshold, Mr. Poroshenko avoided the need for a runoff ballot. Every previous Presidential election since Ukraine regained independence had to go to a second round.

Two other things were notable in the election results. First, of the top five candidates, four—who together won a combined total of 77 percent of the vote—supported Ukraine drawing closer to the European Union. Second, in contrast to all the talk in Russia of neofascists running things in Ukraine, the two candidates from far right parties won a combined total of less than 2 percent of the vote.

DOMESTIC CHALLENGES

Mr. Poroshenko will be sworn in as Ukraine's fifth President on Saturday.

Eastern Ukraine poses the first of several difficult challenges awaiting him. Dozens, if not hundreds, have died in clashes between Ukrainian military and security forces and armed separatists in Donetsk and Luhansk over the past month. Mr. Poroshenko has said his first trip as President will be to Donetsk.

Many in eastern Ukraine are troubled by how government power in Kiev changed in February and regard the acting government as illegitimate. Polls show, however, that more than 70 percent wish to remain a part of Ukraine. Mr. Poroshenko's election should lift some of that cloud of illegitimacy. If he can successfully assure the population in the east that he will listen to and address their political and economic concerns, he can undercut support for the armed separatists, whose welcome may be wearing out. That could also give a boost to the roundtable process launched by the Organization for Security and Cooperation in Europe aimed at resolving Ukraine's internal divisions.

Mr. Poroshenko's second challenge will be implementing the economic reforms to which Ukraine agreed in order to receive $17 billion in low-interest loans from the International Monetary Fund over the next 2 years. Ukraine has the potential to receive as much as $25–$35 billion from the International Monetary Fund, other international financial institutions and Western governments to help it meet its external debt obligations—provided that it implements its reform program.

The reforms are necessary to put the country's economic house in order and end rampant corruption. But the reforms will hurt many households across the country. Mr. Poroshenko will need to find a way to sustain the public's support for pursuing those reforms, a potentially difficult political test.

The third challenge is decentralizing Ukraine's Government, in which too much power rests in the capital. Transferring some political authority to the oblasts—such as making regional governors elected as opposed to appointed by the President—would promote more effective, efficient, and accountable governance. It would also address demands in the eastern part of the country for more local authority.

Mr. Poroshenko has said that he would like to see early Rada (Parliament) elections this year. That would be a wise move, as it would revalidate the Rada's democratic legitimacy in the aftermath of February's turmoil and would put in place Rada deputies reflecting the country's current mood.

With regard to foreign policy, Mr. Poroshenko supports bringing Ukraine closer to the European Union, which includes signing a Ukraine-EU association agreement that contains a deep and comprehensive free trade arrangement. That will expand access to EU markets for Ukrainian exporters. Opinion polls show that a majority of Ukrainians supports a pro-European Union course.

Mr. Poroshenko has also expressed a desire to develop a working relationship with Russia—a sensible position given the many links and interactions between Ukraine and Russia. The principal challenge, however, is that Mr. Putin and the Kremlin oppose Ukraine's pro-Europe course, which would remove the country from Russia's sphere of influence. There are no significant indications to suggest that Moscow's goal of holding Ukraine back from Europe has changed.

RUSSIA'S APPROACH AND MOTIVES

On May 23, Mr. Putin said he would respect the results of the Ukrainian Presidential election. If Moscow is prepared to deal directly with Kiev in a normal manner and cease its support for the separatists who have created chaos in Donetsk and Luhansk, that would be a positive and welcome step. But skepticism is in order: this would amount to a total reversal in Russia's course over the past 3 months—and it is not clear why the Kremlin now would decide to do that.

Kiev, the United States and European Union will watch closely to see how Russia deals with Mr. Poroshenko in the coming weeks. After 2 months of intimidating military maneuvers on Ukraine's eastern border, it appears that Russia now has finally returned most of the troops to their bases. That is a welcome step.

Russia has legitimate interests in Ukraine. But those interests do not mean that it should resort to force, seize Ukrainian territory, and support separatism. There is much that the Russians could do if they truly wished to defuse the crisis. There are many indicators that the Russian Government has been supporting the armed separatists in eastern Ukraine, including by providing leadership, such as Colonel Chirkin (Strelkov). The Russian Government could end that support and order its personnel to cease fighting. Moscow has taken no visible steps to urge the separatists in eastern Ukraine to lay down arms and evacuate occupied buildings, as was agreed in Geneva in mid-April. It could do so now. The flow of arms, including sophisticated antiaircraft weapons, other supplies and fighters, including from Chechnya, continues from Russia into eastern Ukraine. That is something Russian border guards could interdict if ordered to do so.

Mr. Putin's approach toward Ukraine thus far appears driven by several factors.

Russia's main focus has not been Crimea, which it illegally occupied in March. The Kremlin appears to seek a weak and compliant Ukrainian neighbor, a state that will defer to Moscow and not develop a significant relationship with the European Union. For Mr. Putin, possessing Crimea while mainland Ukraine draws closer to Europe is no victory.

Although he lamented the collapse of the Soviet Union as the greatest geopolitical catastrophe of the 20th century, Mr. Putin does not seek to rebuild it. Doing so would require that Russia subsidize the economies of others, an economic burden that Moscow does not wish to bear.

What Mr. Putin does want is a sphere of influence, which he views as a key component of Moscow's great power status. Countries within that sphere are expected to eschew policies, such as drawing too close to NATO or the European Union, that the Kremlin regards as inconsistent with Russian interests. A Ukraine that has signed, and is implementing, an EU association agreement would be a country moving irretrievably out of Moscow's geopolitical orbit.

Domestic political factors also motivate Mr. Putin's policy. The seizure of Crimea was popular with most Russians, particularly his conservative political base. His domestic approval rating now exceeds 80 percent. Trying to pull Ukraine back toward Russia, given the historical and cultural links, is also popular with many Russians.

Another factor apparently motivating Mr. Putin is to see the Maidan experiment—which began with the demonstrations that started in late November and continues as Ukraine shapes a new government—fail. As was evident in 2012 following the brief period of large demonstrations in Moscow, the Kremlin greatly fears civil protest and moved quickly to clamp down. It does not want to see protest succeed in neighboring Ukraine.

Finally, while it is difficult to understand how the Kremlin functions, some suggest that Mr. Putin operates in a bubble in which he receives information from relatively narrow channels dominated by the security services. When the Russian President talks about what has happened in Ukraine over the past 6 months—or about what happened 10 years ago during the Orange Revolution—he does not describe protests motivated by popular discontent with an increasingly authoritarian leadership or a stolen election. He sees an effort orchestrated and led by the CIA and its sister European services, aimed in large part at hemming in Russia. Such a flawed understanding of Ukraine is worrisome, as bad analysis offers a poor foundation on which to base policy.

How will Russia proceed regarding Ukraine? The April 17 meeting of the U.S., Russian, Ukrainian and European Union Foreign Ministers offered a chance for a diplomatic solution. Little appears to have come of it. Moscow did nothing to get illegal armed groups in cities such as Donetsk or Slavyansk to disarm or evacuate the buildings that they occupied. Instead, it appears to have encouraged and supported those groups. Today, unfortunately, the Russians continue to do little to exercise the very considerable authority that they have with the armed separatists to defuse the crisis.

It is not clear that Mr. Putin has a grand strategy on Ukraine. He may be making decisions on an ad hoc basis. He likely did not decide to move to seize Crimea, for example, until he saw how events played out in Kiev at the end of February. He then saw an opportunity, and he took it.

We must bear in mind that Mr. Putin surprised the West. Once it became clear that the acting government in Kiev would pursue the EU association agreement, most analysts expected a negative reaction from Moscow. But we anticipated that Russia would resort to its considerable economic leverage: block Ukrainian exports to Russia, press for payment of outstanding loans, or raise the price of natural gas for Ukraine. Russia instead used its military to take Crimea.

The West should also bear in mind Mr. Putin's claim to a right to protect Russian ''compatriots''—ethnic Russians and Russian-speakers who do not have Russian citizenship. This was the justification for Russian action in Crimea. What does it mean for other states neighboring Russia with significant ethnic Russian minority populations?

THE U.S. POLICY RESPONSE

The U.S. policy response over the past 3 months appears to have three vectors: support Ukraine, reassure NATO allies, and penalize Russia with the goal of effecting a change in Moscow's policy.

The first vector has aimed to bolster Ukraine. Since the acting government took office in late February, there has been a steady stream of senior U.S. officials to Kiev, including Deputy Secretary of State Bill Burns, Secretary of State John Kerry, and Vice President Joe Biden. The Vice President will return to Kiev for Mr. Poroshenko's inauguration. President Obama has hosted Acting Prime Minister Arseniy Yatseniuk and met Mr. Poroshenko yesterday during his visit to Warsaw. These demonstrate U.S. political support and bolster the Government in Kiev.

The United States worked closely with the International Monetary Fund to develop the current program for Ukraine. Provided that Ukraine implements the program's reforms, it is front-loaded to give Ukraine early access to significant funds, much more so than in most 2-year IMF programs. U.S. assistance programs should now focus on helping Ukraine implement the agreed reforms.

U.S. officials have launched particular programs to assist Ukraine. Of particular importance is the effort to help Ukraine diversify its energy sources and increase energy efficiency so that it can reduce its dependence on Russia. A second program seeks to help Ukraine track where funds stolen by officials in the previous government went, with the goal of freezing and securing the return of those moneys to Ukraine.

One area where the United States should do more is military assistance. The Ukrainian military needs help in strengthening its defensive capabilities. Given that most Ukrainian army bases are in the western part of the country—a legacy of Soviet times when Soviet forces in Ukraine were deployed primarily against NATO—many units that deployed to Donetsk and Luhansk lack infrastructure. MREs and other nonlethal equipment such as sleeping bags, tents, and logistics are needed to help sustain soldiers in the field.

The decision to provide body armor, night-vision goggles, and communications equipment is welcome, if overdue. The United States should also offer counterinsurgency advice and intelligence support. It is appropriate to consider providing light antiarmor weapons and man-portable air defense systems, particularly since the Ukrainian military, at U.S. and NATO request, eliminated many of its man-portable air defense systems so that they would not be subject to possible theft and terrorist use. Finally, the U.S. military should continue its program of exercises with the Ukrainian military, which has been a standard element of the U.S.-Ukraine military-to-military cooperation program for more than 15 years.

The second vector of U.S. policy has been to reassure NATO allies in the Baltic and Central European regions, who are more nervous about Moscow's intentions and possible actions following the seizure of Crimea. U.S. and NATO military forces have deployed to the regions with the objectives of reassuring those allies of the alliance's commitment to their defense and of underscoring that commitment to Moscow.

The most significant deployment has been that of four U.S. airborne companies, one each to Estonia, Latvia, Lithuania, and Poland, for what the Pentagon has described as a ''persistent'' deployment. These units lack heavy weapons and pose no offensive threat to Russia, but they are a tangible indicator of U.S. commitment to the four allies. It would send an even stronger message were the U.S. companies joined by companies from other alliance members. For example, a German company might be paired with the U.S. company in Lithuania, a British company with the U.S. company in Estonia, and so on.

Speaking on Tuesday in Warsaw, President Obama proposed a $1 billion program to increase the U.S. military presence in Central Europe. This is an appropriate step, given new concerns about Russia and Russian policy since the Kremlin's seizure of Crimea. Congress should approve expedited funding for this.

The third vector of U.S. policy has to been to penalize Russia with the goal of effecting a change in Moscow's course on Ukraine. Washington has ratcheted down bilateral relations, and G7 leaders—the G8 less Mr. Putin—met today in Brussels instead of in Sochi, as had originally been planned.

The U.S. Government has worked with the European Union to impose visa and financial sanctions on selected individuals and entities over the past 2 months. While the Russian economy was already weakening in 2013, the sanctions imposed to date, although modest, appear to be having an impact.

The Russian Finance Minister has projected that Russian GDP growth in 2014 would be ½ percent at most and perhaps zero. That is down from projections of 2.0–2.5 percent in 2013. The Russian Economy Minister said that the Russian economy could be in recession by June, a development that he attributed to geopolitical circumstances, i.e., the effects of Russian policy toward Ukraine and the resulting sanctions.

The Russian Finance Minister also noted that capital flight in the first quarter of 2014 amounted to $50 billion. Other sources suggest it was higher, perhaps on the order of $60–70 billion. Standard & Poor's has reduced the investment grade of sovereign Russian debt to one level above junk bond status. According to Bloomberg, no Russian company has been able to sell foreign currency bonds since March, in contrast to 2013, when Russian companies sold $42.5 billion worth of such bonds.

The sanctions are having an economic impact, but they thus far have failed in their primary purpose. Russia has not significantly altered its course on Ukraine.

The U.S. Government has been more restrained than it should have on sanctions. Part of the reason is the administration's desire to move in concert with the European Union, so as to minimize the opportunity for Russian wedge-driving or selectively targeting American companies for retaliation. Unfortunately, the European Union has been overly cautious on sanctions, in large part due to concern for its trade with Russia, which is more than 10 times U.S.-Russia trade, and the need to find consensus among 28 member states, which generally produces a lowest common denominator approach.

The West needs to recognize that Moscow remains part of the problem in Ukraine and is not yet part of the solution. Absent a change in the Russian course, the United States and European Union should apply further and more robust sanctions, which are already more than justified by Russia's actions. Additional sanctions could include:

- Expanding the list of individual Russians—inside and outside of government—targeted for visa and financial sanctions. Sanctions should apply to family members as well.
- Applying targeted sanctions on the Russian financial sector, beginning with the sanctioning of at least one major Russian financial institution (as opposed to smaller pocket banks).
- Blocking Western energy companies from new investments to develop oil and gas fields in Russia, just as the United States and European Union have moved to block their companies from investing in the development of oil and gas resources on the Black Sea shelf around Crimea.

The goal of sanctions should be to change Mr. Putin's calculus. Russian analysts have long described an implicit social contract that he has with the Russian people: diminished individual political space in return for economic stability, growth and rising living standards. He delivered spectacularly on his part of the bargain from 2000–2008, when the Russian economy grew by seven-eight percent per year. Some Russian economists in 2013 questioned, however, whether the projected 2.0–2.5 percent growth would suffice; the objective of sanctions should be to inflict economic pain on Russia and undermine Mr. Putin's ability to deliver on his side of the bargain. That may—may, not necessarily will—lead him to adopt a new policy course.

There is an alternative view. It holds that Mr. Putin will use the sanctions as a scapegoat and attempt to put all the blame on the West for Russia's poor economic performance. How sanctions will affect the Russian public's view toward Mr. Putin and his calculations regarding policy regarding Ukraine remain to be seen. The egregious nature of Russian actions over the past several months nevertheless argues that the West should impose significant consequences.

In considering and applying sanctions, the U.S. Government should be smart. Where possible, it makes sense to use a scalpel and carefully target sanctions rather than a sledgehammer. It also makes sense to avoid policies that would not help Ukraine and would damage other U.S. interests—such as halting implementation of the New START treaty or accelerating the deployment of SM–3 missile interceptors that may not be technically ready for deployment in Poland.

POSSIBLE ELEMENTS OF A SETTLEMENT

Washington should encourage Kiev to pull together the strands of a package to stabilize its internal situation, including elements of interest to many in eastern Ukraine. Elements of a settlement could include the following:

De-escalation of the fighting in eastern Ukraine. The Ukrainian military could cease security operations if the armed separatist groups stand down and negotiate an evacuation of the buildings that they have occupied over the past 2 months. Moscow has called on Kiev to halt its operations; it could greatly increase the chances of this if it persuaded the separatists to abide by the Geneva agreement to evacuate occupied buildings and disarm. For its part, the government in Kiev should disarm the far-right Praviy Sektor movement.

Decentralization of political authority. Members of the acting government and Mr. Poroshenko have suggested the possibility that some political authority could be shifted from Kiev to regional and local leaders. Mr. Poroshenko should put forward concrete proposals for decentralization, which may require constitutional reform. One obvious step would be to make the oblast governors elected as opposed to appointed by the President. It would also be sensible to transfer some budget authority to regional governments.

Early Rada elections. The May 25 Presidential election gives Mr. Poroshenko a strong democratic mandate. It would make sense to hold early Rada elections in order to renew the democratic legitimacy of the parliamentary body as well.

Russian language status. The acting government has indicated its readiness to give the Russian language official status (which it already enjoys in certain regions as the result of a language law passed during the Yanukovych Presidency). Mr. Poroshenko could affirm his readiness to support official status for Russian.

International relations. Kiev's foreign policy is of interest to many Ukrainians. Some, as well as Russia, are concerned about the prospect of deepening relations between Ukraine and NATO, despite the fact that the acting government and Mr. Poroshenko have indicated that they have no desire to draw closer to NATO. That is and should be Kiev's decision. But not pursuing a deeper relationship with NATO now seems an appropriate policy for Ukraine: deepening relations with NATO would antagonize Moscow, and there is no appetite in the alliance to accept Ukraine as a member or offer a membership action plan. Most importantly, a push toward NATO would be hugely divisive within Ukraine, where polls show at most only 20–30 percent of the population would support such a policy; it would be particularly controversial in eastern Ukraine. Without forever foreclosing the option, Kiev should be able to articulate a position that assures Russia that NATO is not in the cards in the near- or medium-term, a policy that the alliance could acknowledge.

Mr. Poroshenko, the Rada and a majority of Ukrainians favor drawing closer to the European Union and signing the Ukraine-EU association agreement. Moscow has complained that the European Union refused last year to discuss with it the association agreement. Kiev might indicate that it would be prepared for a trilateral EU-Ukraine-Russia discussion on steps that the European Union and Ukraine could take to ameliorate negative effects of the association agreement on Ukraine-Russia trade—but not on the question of Ukraine's right to decide for itself whether or not to sign the agreement.

Crimea. It is very difficult to envisage a scenario by which Ukraine regains sovereignty over Crimea. That does not mean that Ukraine or the West should accept Russia's illegal occupation and annexation. However, in a broader dialogue to find a settlement, it might make sense for Kiev and Moscow to set Crimea aside for the time being and return to the issue later after a settlement of other issues has been reached.

These elements, which build on many points that the acting Ukrainian Government and Mr. Poroshenko have already articulated, could provide a basis for stabilizing Ukraine. They address a number of issues that the Russians have raised over the past 3 months—though they do not go as far as Moscow would want. The big question is whether the Kremlin would be prepared to support any settlement that shaped up along the above lines. At the moment, it is not clear that the Russians would.

CONCLUSION

Mr. Chairman, Senator Corker, members of the committee, the Ukraine crisis will likely continue for some time to come. With the election of a new President, the government in Kiev is better prepared to meet the challenges confronting it than was the case 3 weeks ago. Still, the challenges are steep.

Addressing those challenges would be substantially easier were Russia to cease its efforts to destabilize Ukraine and adopt a more helpful policy. But it does not appear that the Kremlin is ready to cease those destabilization efforts. If it does not, the United States and European Union should move to apply more robust sanctions on Russia, with the goal of persuading Moscow to change its policy.

International financial institutions and Western governments have pulled together a substantial financial package for Ukraine. The United States and European Union should target their assistance programs to help the Ukrainian Government implement the economic reforms in its IMF program. That will help Kiev stay on program—necessary for continued access to international financing—and will help bring about the reforms needed to build a more transparent, competitive, and productive economy.

Washington should also encourage the Ukrainian Government to develop a settlement package that would help heal the internal differences that have developed over the past 4 months. Once Kiev adopts that package, the United States and European Union should give it full political backing and urge the Russians to support it as well.

Stabilizing Ukraine will take time. But it has rich economic potential and a talented people. Many Ukrainians seem to recognize that they have a precious second chance to turn their country around—after the missed opportunity of the Orange Revolution.

U.S. and Western policy should aim to maximize the prospects that, this time, Ukraine will succeed. That will be important for the people of Ukraine and for a more stable and secure Europe. Also, the best rebuke to the Kremlin's policy would be to see Ukraine in several years' time looking more and more like Poland—a normal, democratic, rule of law, and increasingly prosperous European state.

The CHAIRMAN. Thank you.
Ambassador Jeffrey.

STATEMENT OF HON. JAMES F. JEFFREY, PHILIP SOLONDZ DISTINGUISHED VISITING FELLOW, THE WASHINGTON INSTITUTE; FORMER ASSISTANT TO THE PRESIDENT AND DEPUTY NATIONAL SECURITY ADVISOR, WASHINGTON, DC

Ambassador JEFFREY. Thank you very much, Mr. Chairman, Senator Corker, members of the committee. Again, I very much appreciate being here today.

The Russian aggression against Ukraine is the most serious challenge to the international order since 9/11. As such, this crisis requires action at three levels.

The first of the immediate steps that have been taken and are being taken deal with the phenomenon itself. As the acting National Security Advisor with President Bush during the 2008 invasion of Georgia, I believe that the administration, under somewhat similar circumstances, had done, all in all, a good job dealing with the Russian incursion into Crimea and now in eastern Ukraine. It has not challenged Russia militarily on the ground, and I think that is a wise decision given the stakes and given the difficulty of deploying U.S. troops. On the other hand, it has used economic sanctions and every diplomatic tool possible and, in particular, brought along an initially recalcitrant Europe. And this will be a problem going forward as well, but the administration is trying its best on that.

Thanks to both these efforts by the international community and, more importantly, as my colleagues have noted, the will of the Ukrainian people represented in the elections and the willingness of people even in eastern Ukraine to support a unified and sovereign Ukraine, the Russians have had to change their tactics somewhat, less direct military aggression, more indirect forces. But, nonetheless, as my Foreign Service colleague, Steve Pifer, just said, the strategy that Putin is following remains the same: to destabilize Ukraine and ensure it can never be a sovereign country able to choose its own future, which I believe would be with the West, and defend itself against falling under Russian sway.

Thus, at the second level, we need to look at additional steps. The administration has announced a number of good moves this week. The Senate in the draft Preventing Russian Aggression bill has come up with others. I have my own. I will just touch on a few.

First of all, I would second Ambassador Pifer. We need to provide not just MREs, although they are needed, but weapons and advisory teams to help the Ukrainians deal with this insurgency in the east. We have much experience in stability operations. They need to know how to use military force while reaching out to the population.

Secondly, we need to, as the President said, very rapidly deploy significant heavy—that is, armor-heavy—prepositioned stocks and rotational forces along the borders of NATO's east. Again, the President is moving forward on this. This should not wait for additional money. We have the equipment. We can deploy the troops. We should also ensure that this becomes a NATO mission and that NATO also provides troops along with ours, as we did several times during the cold war.

We have mentioned economic support for Ukraine. That's very, very important. And there, President Poroshenko is going to have to do a lot of work himself because a lot of money has gone into Ukraine without much result.

Finally, as mentioned in your draft bill, we need to do more to wean Europe from Russian gas and from Russian financial investments and other pressures that it is able to use thanks to its economy. There are ways to do this that would have immediate and, more importantly, long-term effects. The long-term issue I want to dwell on for a little bit because that's the third order of magnitude we have here.

Again, what we have seen in the last months is an extraordinary development in the history of Europe and certainly in the history of the post-cold war. I reject the notion that Russia was pushed into this by NATO's expansion east. I was involved at a certain level on those decisions back 20 years ago, and while perhaps that could have been done differently, the point is as NATO moved east, it also stood down the vast majority of its conventional forces. Russia did not do the same. The United States, the EU, the international community tried for 20 years with tens of billions of dollars to integrate Russia into the international community in every way possible. The result is a Russia that is trying to expand again using 18th century models.

At this point, we have to consider the stark likelihood of not just a Russia but possibly a China as well, ever more closely tied to

Russia, motivated to challenge both the international order and America as guarantor of that system. We need to start thinking as a country, as an alliance, and as a global community about the implications of this. If we wish to avoid a geostrategic shift, as dramatic as 1989 only in the other direction, maintaining the integrity of this international order including, if needed, by force must be among our vital interests.

Thank you very much, Senators.

[The prepared statement of Ambassador Jeffrey follows:]

PREPARED STATEMENT OF AMBASSADOR JAMES F. JEFFREY

Chairman Menendez, Ranking Member Corker, and members of the committee, thank you for inviting me here today. What has happened in Ukraine is the most significant challenge to the international order since the attacks of September 11. While not aimed directly at the United States, the strategic fallout of Russia's aggression against Ukraine is, in some respects, more threatening to the global order we have helped build and defend over the past century. After all, we are not dealing with a terrorist group, but a nuclear-armed U.N. Security Council permanent member, one of the world's greatest hydrocarbons exporters, intending to regain the international status enjoyed by the Soviet Union. To this end, Russia has used all tools at its disposal, from gas export blackmail to direct and indirect invasion—from Georgia and Syria to Crimea and Eastern Ukraine—to achieve that status, not only trampling the values that ground our global order in the process, but to a significant degree, attempting to replace it.

As such, the Ukraine crisis requires action at three levels by the United States and its partners. First, we must take immediate steps to deal with the situation at hand in a Ukraine being deliberately destabilized. Second, we must take long-term steps to counter the Russian goal of denying Ukraine any level of independence and stability that would permit it to develop relations with the West and avoid being absorbed by Russia. Third, Russian actions in Ukraine and elsewhere, combined with China's actions in its near abroad, and the ever-deepening partnership of Russia and China, require us and our friends to rethink the very foundations of the international order since 1989.

The Obama administration has been generally successful at the first level and is working hard at the second, but appears at best uncertain about the third. Let me describe each of these challenges and responses.

Based on my experience with President Bush during Russia's attack on Georgia in 2008, the Obama administration has reacted in a generally reasonable way, similar to that of the Bush administration, to this latest Russian aggression. It has of course had to adapt to an EU often reluctant to act against Russia. It has, correctly, not challenged Russia militarily on an issue of vital importance to it but not directly to us, in an area not easily accessible for U.S. forces. But, as President Obama noted at West Point, his administration has mobilized international condemnation, economic sanctions, albeit limited, and significant coordination with EU states in response, and effectively assisted the new Ukrainian Government. The President has taken appropriate military steps to reinforce NATO's eastern marches, including ship transits into the Black Sea, aircraft reinforcements, and rotating ground troop deployments throughout at least the rest of this year.

These steps have had impact. While sanctions so far have been very limited, their very specter has at least temporarily damaged the Russian economy, from the value of the ruble and investment outflows to GDP growth, and the threat of more sanctions appears to be an effective deterrent against new direct Russian aggression. Furthermore, Mr. Putin did not count on the power of free men and women to act against vassalage. The high turnout and resounding victory of Mr. Poroshenko in the elections 10 days ago, and the reluctance of even many Ukrainians in alleged ''pro-Russian'' areas of Eastern Ukraine to abandon their country, have stymied, at least temporarily, Putin's gambit for an easy, ''popular'' win.

Nevertheless, he has not abandoned his goal ''by other means.'' While Russia has pulled back many of its conventional troops arrayed on the Ukrainian border, its public line concerning the Ukrainian Government remains harsh and dismissive, and it shows no willingness to reverse its illegal annexation of Crimea. Most disturbingly, its continued direct pressure on Kiev—with deployment of irregular combat units to Ukraine to augment Russian nationalists and intelligence teams, and additional financial and gas price pressure—demonstrates that only the tactics, not the goals, of its campaign against Ukraine have changed.

It is thus critical that the United States, NATO, and the EU augment longer term measures to counter this blatant Russian aggression. Many of these measures parallel the proposals in the draft Russian Aggression Prevention Act under consideration. Given the absolute requirement for the United States to act in accordance with NATO and the EU in responding to the Ukraine crisis, I would urge that the administration be given latitude in deciding which measures to implement, how, and when, to ensure we remain synchronized with our European partners. But I believe that the most important steps for the United States and its friends to take should include the following:

- First, lift the ban on lethal weapons and advisory support, including against irregular forces, to the Ukrainian security forces. This is a difficult decision given its impact on Ukrainian Government perceptions, Russian calculations, and European concerns. But refusing direct assistance to a democratic government facing what is unquestionably aggression is a mistake. In the end, such a move almost certainly will not ''provoke'' Putin. He is opting for aggression with or without U.S. ''provocations,'' and while all such steps have risk, we are more likely to gain his attention if we stop ''self-deterring'' ourselves. The Ukrainians have earned the right for more support than MREs. To quote the Fall 2004 edition of Middle East Quarterly, providing an account of the 2004 battle of Kut, Iraq, ''The Ukrainian Army . . . soldiers who were stationed at the CPA compound fought valiantly and tirelessly during the assault.''
- Second, in line with the President's new initiative announced in Warsaw, strengthen NATO's eastern border countries, not simply with deployments of U.S. light infantry, but by prepositioning battalion-size ''heavy packages'' of tanks, infantry fighting vehicles, and self-propelled artillery in each of the frontline NATO states. The United States would keep a company forward deployed with the remainder of a battalion ready to fall in on the prepositioned equipment. This should be a NATO-blessed deployment, and NATO states should provide a second battalion package in each country. That, plus urgent specialized equipping and training of several local battalions in each country to cooperate closely with this force, would give an almost immediately available reinforced heavy brigade on each NATO country's borders. Aside from the significant defensive enhancement against any new ''Crimea,'' this step would signal Moscow that the United States and NATO are going to defend alliance territory, and that military moves are still in the Obama administration's quiver.
- Third, help meet the needs of the Ukrainian economy and its energy sector, along with EU international financial institutions. The IMF has pledged $17 billion, which will be supported by $15 billion from the EU, $1 billion from the United States, and various other sources. This money must be used more wisely by Ukrainians than in the past, but the need is palpable. Providing Ukraine with gas from the European gas net and other energy relief being worked on by the EU and the U.S. Government is critical, especially by the fall.
- Fourth, Ukrainian democracy and unity must be encouraged in the U.N. and other institutions, and on the ground. This means support and counsel in the struggle to regain territory taken by separatists. The United States has much experience in stabilization under fire and should help. The Organization for Security and Cooperation in Europe (OSCE) with its Geneva process is assisting on reconciliation with those among the separatists willing to lay down arms and talk. We should encourage Ukraine to reach out to them. But regaining security control is paramount in contested areas, and we need to help.
- Fifth, keep the sanctions already in place until Russia ceases its attempts to subvert Ukraine and is willing to discuss the future of Crimea.
- Sixth, help Western Europe become less dependent on Russian gas and cash flows. Overall trade and financial exchanges with Russia are limited for the EU, but significant for Russia. That theoretically gives the EU the upper hand. But Russia is a command economy with one man deciding. Europe is a decentralized capitalist economy, with many vested interests and no single leader. Thus, this will not be easy. Nevertheless, initiatives to give Europe more energy options— including steps to realize what the Economist estimates as a possible U.S. export of 75 billion cubic meters of gas a year and other measures to promote liquefied natural gas—must have priority.

But, while Ukraine's fate is not yet secured and will be a risk even with these measures, my biggest concern is at the aforementioned third level, the underlying message that Putin's many moves against the global order portend.

While on the margins the United States and NATO could have tailored relations with Russia differently since 1991, I reject the notion that it was Western actions that produced the Russia we face today. Could NATO have decided not to expand eastward? Of course, but it is difficult to see how that would have assuaged Putin and at least a good part of the Russian population who long for the return of a Soviet-sized empire. After all, while NATO expanded, it simultaneously drew down dramatically. U.S. combat brigade equivalents in Europe are down from 18 in 1989 to 2 today. Major continental NATO armies, notably the British, German, and French, have been drastically cut, with conscription ended. The Russian military to the contrary has not been reduced proportionally. NATO expansion thus did not increase an alliance offensive threat against Russia. Rather, it strove to block the re-creation of Imperial and Soviet Russia through force, an inherently legitimate goal existential to the free peoples of eastern Europe.

Furthermore, throughout the last 20-plus years the United States, NATO, the EU, OSCE, and other international organizations did everything possible to fashion for Russia a strategic position in the global order, from tens of billions of dollars in direct and indirect aid, to massive investments and joint ventures, to subcontracting much of Western European energy requirements to Gazprom, to sponsoring Russian entry into Western global institutions, most notably the World Trade Organization, and reinforcing the Security Council. Clearly neither that nor the drawdown of NATO force structure had any effect on Putin and many of his countrymen and women. Rather, it is at least as likely that by providing him with potential pressure points from gas deliveries to local conventional-force superiority, it encouraged his policies.

At this point, we have to consider the stark likelihood of not just a Russia, but possibly a China as well, motivated to challenge both the international order based on peaceful settlement of disputes, international law, and global security, and America as guarantor of that system. If, as is likely based on events from Crimea to the South China Sea, this threat materializes, the United States will have to rethink its entire foreign policy.

Neither Europe, as we have seen repeatedly in the current Ukraine crisis, nor Japan and South Korea, are able on their own to "pivot" to a new posture. This will require analysis and then action by the United States. This potential threat was not covered in detail in the President's West Point speech. Furthermore, his recipe for most foreign policy challenges—acting only with the support and concurrence of international organizations, and within multilateral constraints—is unlikely to work against major conventional state competitors. For example, such an approach certainly will be impossible at least in the U.N. with Russia and China at the table, and very difficult with the EU or with our East Asian allies without strong, "from the front" U.S. leadership, including readiness to use force to defend the current system. The administration appears ambivalent about such uses of force. But if we wish to avoid a geostrategic shift as dramatic as 1989, only in the other direction, then maintaining the integrity of this global system must be among our "vital" interests.

The CHAIRMAN. Ambassador Green.

STATEMENT OF HON. MARK GREEN, PRESIDENT, INTERNATIONAL REPUBLICAN INSTITUTE; FORMER U.S. AMBASSADOR; AND MEMBER, U.S. HOUSE OF REPRESENTATIVES, WASHINGTON, DC

Ambassador GREEN. Thank you, Mr. Chairman. Chairman Menendez, Senator Corker, members of the committee, I appreciate this opportunity to testify on recent developments in Ukraine. I will summarize my written testimony and try not to repeat what others have said.

IRI's mission is to encourage democracy in places where it is absent, help democracy become more effective where it is in danger, and share best practices where democracy is flourishing. Given that mission, it is only natural that Ukraine has been an essential part of our programming for more than 20 years. In addition to our primary office in Kiev, we have operated offices in Odessa and, until recently, in Crimea.

IRI has monitored all national elections in independent Ukraine's history, including the most recent election on May 25. Our high-level mission was led by Senator Kelly Ayotte, your colleague, and included Congressman Peter Roskam, chairman of the House Democracy Partnership. We visited more than 100 polling stations in places like Cherkasy, Kharkiv, and Odessa. In preparation for this election, we trained more than 5,000 observers representing candidates, political parties, and the Maidan movement.

In the view of our observation team, these elections were free and fair and met international standards. Of course, what makes their accomplishment so remarkable is the wide range of challenges Ukrainian officials faced while administering this election. In many ways, these challenges remain and need urgent attention—and perhaps the help of the West.

As others have noted, one very obvious challenge they faced in recent months was Russian-sponsored violence in the south and east. Separatists used high-grade, cutting-edge tactics and equipment. There were widespread cases of these violent groups taking over radio stations, establishing checkpoints, and in one case, shutting down an airport. Well-equipped bands of military style forces sought to shut down the election in parts of the country, and in a few places they succeeded.

Another challenge that was and is important and that I do not think has received enough attention is the plight and tragedy of Crimean Tatars. The history of suffering of the Tatar people is well-known. Stalin's forced deportation resulted in the death of tens of thousands of Tatars, and they were only able to return to their ancestral homeland near the end of the Soviet Union. They now make up nearly 15 percent of Crimean's population. They have boycotted the illegal Crimean March referendum and rejected its results, and the community has repeatedly pledged its continued support for a united and sovereign Ukraine. Obviously, their courage might not have the approval of Moscow.

Since the beginning of our work in Ukraine, we have sought to assist the democratic aspirations of the Crimean Tatar people. We have worked with them closely to build communication exchanges and to try to link them up, particularly youth, with Western Europe and other parts of Ukraine. Unfortunately, we are unable to continue that programming in occupied Crimea, and we would very much like to return and find ways to help this population. In any case, in light of the Russian annexation and the Soviet history, we should all be very watchful of how the Tatars are able to live and work and hopefully prosper in the face of Russian rule.

In some ways, the most serious challenge Ukraine is facing, I would argue, is the overwhelming force of Russian propaganda that has been projected into that country, combined with the lack of Ukrainian media and social media in certain areas. It is hard for any nation to build a sense of national purpose and unity when there is a lack of indigenous media. It is nearly impossible when that void is filled with hostile, foreign-born propaganda bent on destabilizing communities and government borders. We should work to help foster independent, truly Ukraine-centered media that can reach out to every part of that country. More and more people, especially young people, now get their news and information through social media platforms. Again, there's a lack of social media platforms that are Ukraine-centered in parts of that country, and I do believe that we can help boost social media platforms that will help create a sense of unity and identity.

One of the most subtle and yet serious, challenges that Ukraine has faced, and will continue to face, is a weakened IT infrastructure. Recent reports suggest that much of the government's IT has been compromised by foreign-sponsored viruses. On the day of the election, the IRI delegation learned that Russia had launched a major cyber attack aimed at bringing down the Central Election Commission's main database. Had it succeeded, the elections would have failed and perhaps given Ukraine's opponents further pretense for mischief, aggression and destabilizing activities. In this day and age, effective IT is absolutely necessary for effective democracy and governance.

Members of the committee, it is too easy to focus on their challenges in Ukraine. We should also focus on the hopeful signs. As my colleague, Jane Harman, has noted, President-elect Poroshenko has already taken significant steps to move the country forward. He has indicated that he will retain current Prime Minister Yatsenyuk and some other members in the current government. He stated his top priorities are to maintain the unity of the country by reaching out to the eastern regions, tackling corruption and creating jobs.

Mr. Chairman, recent events in Ukraine make clear both the challenges and possibilities that lie ahead. The fact that Ukrainians, in the span of a few short months were able to remove from office a corrupt but powerful leader and then turn around and conduct national elections that met international standards is remarkable. The fact that all of this was accomplished in the face of threats and violence is historic.

To be clear, as my former colleague, Jane Harman, has said, the Ukrainians, not their friends in the West, are responsible for shaping their country's future. They have a unique history and a rich culture that is all their own. They want to chart a path that meets their own needs and aspirations, not anyone else's. As one of IRI's Ukrainian staff proudly said to us recently, "We went to the Maidan to find Europe, and instead we found Ukraine." This is a great moment for Ukraine and potentially a great moment for democracy.

Thank you, Mr. Chairman.

[The prepared statement of Ambassador Green follows:]

PREPARED STATEMENT OF HON. MARK GREEN

INTRODUCTION

Chairman Menendez, Senator Corker, members of the Senate Foreign Relations Committee, thank you for this opportunity to testify on recent developments in Ukraine. Given the present challenges facing the Ukrainian people and their newly elected leadership—from rebuilding an economy devastated by corruption and mismanagement to defeating the efforts of a small, but deadly group of foreign-inspired (if not foreign-sponsored) separatists—this hearing is urgently needed. The implications of what is happening in Ukraine, especially in areas near its border with Russia, could affect developments throughout the region.

IRI'S DEEP TIES TO UKRAINE

The International Republican Institute (IRI) is a nonprofit, nonpartisan organization, and one of the four core institutes of the National Endowment for Democracy. Our mission is to encourage democracy in places where it is absent, help democracy become more effective where it is in danger, and share best practices where democracy is flourishing. While Ukraine's future is obviously up to Ukrainians, at IRI, we believe the community of Western democracies can play an indispensable role in providing tools and assistance to help Ukraine realize its great potential.

Ukraine has long been an essential part of IRI's programs. In fact, thanks to the support of numerous funders from the United States, Europe, and Canada, IRI has been operating democracy and governance initiatives there for more than 20 years. In addition to our primary office in Kiev, we have operated offices in Odessa and, until recently, Simferopol in the Crimean Peninsula.

In carrying out our mission to support more democratic, more accountable governance, we have tried to enhance civic engagement and advocacy at the subnational level by increasing civil society organizations' capacity and strengthening their linkages with political parties. We have worked to foster a national dialogue involving civic and political activists from all around the country. For example, we have brought together local elected officials from cities which border Russia and cities in western Ukraine to learn from each other and create a network of reform-oriented leaders. We have sought to increase the participation of youth, women, and minority groups in political processes. (IRI's Women's Democracy Network (WDN), one of our flagship programs, launched a chapter in Ukraine in February 2011. The Ukrainian women of WDN started an innovative gender monitoring project during the 2012 parliamentary election campaign to support women candidates, boost the participation of women in political life, and raise people's awareness about the importance of women's participation in decisionmaking processes at the national level. Later this year, WDN Ukraine will establish a special Political Leadership Academy to develop potential women candidates.)

In particular, over the course of many years, IRI has developed extensive relationships with the Crimean Tatar community. IRI has worked with Tatar civic organizations to enhance their capacity to conduct young political leadership schools and public hearings on the peninsula. IRI was also the only international organization to observe the Tatar community's local elections in 2013.

MAY 25 PRESIDENTIAL ELECTION

IRI has monitored all national elections in independent Ukraine's history, including the most recent Presidential election on May 25. IRI fielded a high-level election observation mission led by Senator Kelly Ayotte and included Congressman Peter Roskam, which visited more than 100 polling stations in Cherkasy, Chernihiv, Dnipropetrovsk, Kharkiv, Kiev, Mykolaiv, Odesa, Ternopil, and Vinnitsya. In preparation for elections, we trained more than 5,000 observers representing candidates, parties, and the Maidan to help ensure the transparency and legitimacy of the electoral process.

IRI observers reported only minor irregularities and none that would affect the outcome of the election. Our observers reported that the election was well-administered and that polling officials were knowledgeable and approached their job seriously, working long hours, without breaks to ensure that the election was free, fair, and democratic. In areas of the country where nearly 87 percent of the population resides, polls were open and voting went smoothly. In the limited areas where voting was denied or suppressed—Crimea, Donetsk, and Luhansk—it was due either to Russian occupation or interference.

In short, in the view of the IRI observation team, these elections were free and fair, and met international standards. What makes this accomplishment especially remarkable is the range of challenges Ukrainian officials faced as they administered this election. Some of the challenges, as described below, will need urgent attention from the Poroshenko government in the months ahead. They also represent opportunities for friends of Ukraine (such as the U.S., Canada and Europe) to help.

VIOLENCE FROM RUSSIA

Among the most obvious challenges that Ukrainian officials have faced in recent months was the Russian-sponsored violence in the south and east. The Russian-sponsored separatists used high-grade, cutting-edge tactics and equipment. There were widespread cases of these groups taking over radio stations, shootings, establishing checkpoints, and in one case, shutting down an airport. Well-equipped bands of military style forces sought to shut down the election in parts of the country, and in a few places they succeeded.

The appearance of Russian-sponsored special forces without insignia or other identification seemed designed to create uncertainty and confusion among military and civilians alike. The use of paid mercenaries, Russian counterintelligence service (GRU) veterans and now, apparently Chechen fighters, presented Ukrainian security leaders with new tactical challenges and, no doubt, will be studied by American and other Western analysts in months to come.

TATARS UNDER RUSSIAN OCCUPATION

Another specific challenge that we at IRI want to bring to the committee's attention is the plight and the tragedy of the Crimean Tatars. Nowhere have the fears of Russian influence been more acutely felt in recent months than in their community in Crimea. The history of the suffering of the Tatar people is well-known. Stalin's deportation resulted in the death of tens of thousands of Tatars. It was not until the final years of the Soviet Union that they were able to finally return to their ancestral homeland. These days, Tatars make up nearly 15 percent of Crimea's population and growing.

The Crimean Tatar community, represented by the Mejlis of the Crimean Tatar people, boycotted the illegal Crimean March 16 referendum and rejected its results. Instead, the community has repeatedly pledged their continued support for a united and sovereign Ukraine. Now their very existence in their homeland is under threat.

Since the beginning of our work in Ukraine, IRI has sought to assist the democratic aspirations of the Crimean Tatar people as they built their own internal democracy within representative bodies such as the Mejlis and the Congress of Crimean Tatar representatives known as the Kurultai. In addition, from 2010 to 2013, IRI conducted a program from our office in Simferopol that sought to equip Crimean Tatars, particularly youth, with the knowledge and skills necessary to enact reforms on the peninsula. IRI also has supported the development of a Web site for the Crimean Tatar Mejlis to improve communications between that body and its community, and conducted a wide range of programming from building the capacity of local Tatar civil society organizations to enabling them to be able to conduct young political leadership schools.

IRI also conducted several exchanges for Tatar youth to travel to other parts of Ukraine and Western Europe to learn from their colleagues and build networks of motivated and politically active youth.

Currently, IRI is unable to conduct programming in occupied Crimea. We would like to find ways to partner with the Crimean Tatar community in the future through a series of study trips for young political and civic activists to both learn from and enhance linkages with their counterparts in other regions of Ukraine. We also see a great need to foster and build independent media on the peninsula. In any case, in light of the Russian annexation and the history of brutal treatment of the Tatars, we should all be watchful of how the Tatars are able to live peacefully and democratically in the face of Russian rule.

RUSSIAN PROPAGANDA, LACK OF UKRAINIAN MEDIA AND SOCIAL MEDIA PLATFORMS

In some ways the most serious challenge facing Ukraine is the overwhelming force of Russian propaganda that has been projected into Ukraine, combined with the lack of Ukrainian media and social media in certain parts of the country. Using English language television in both United States and Europe, the Kremlin has actually convinced many that the invasion and occupation of Crimea was merely an administrative ''correction'' of a Soviet decision made in 1954. It has apparently convinced some in the West that the militants it pays and supplies to create fear and chaos in eastern Ukraine are citizens who feel persecuted due to their ethnicity or language, when polling data completely refutes such assertions. The force and effect of such propaganda is even more pronounced in Ukraine where there is no access to accurate news accounts and analysis at all.

Of course, more and more people, especially young people, get their news and communications through social media platforms. Once again, these channels are currently dominated by Moscow, and countervailing platforms and views are blocked by Moscow wherever they can be. The democracies of the West should help foster free and independent news media in Ukraine that can reach all parts of the country. We should, in particular, support the creation and protection of truly Ukrainian social media that allows users to communicate freely and openly without blockage or intimidation. The recently introduced Russian Aggression Prevention Act has a number of provisions that support these ideas and IRI would welcome the chance to work on this front.

Mr. Chairman, the cold war has been described by many as a conflict of ideals and principles: human rights and free markets versus communism and statism. I would suggest that the West is once again in a conflict, this time with Russia, over ideas and principles. Russia, with an innovative international media program that touts its ''managed democracy'' as the best form of government is making great gains in this battle of ideas. The United States must lead the way in formulating new approaches to counter Russian propaganda. As eloquently stated by former Under Secretary of State Paula Dobriansky. the West must counter Russian President Vladimir Putin's policies and that failure to do so "will embolden Moscow's aggression against other countries with significant Russian populations.''

IT INFRASTRUCTURE AND CYBER WARFARE

One of the most subtle, and yet serious, challenges that Ukraine faced during the election and continues to face today is a weak and, in some cases, infected information technology (IT) infrastructure. In this day and age, people depend on technology for governance, national security, the conduct of elections and many other matters. Recent reports suggest that much of the government's computer structure has been infected or compromised by foreign-sponsored viruses.

On the day of the election, the IRI delegation learned that Russia had launched a major cyber attack aimed at bringing down the Central Election Commission's main database. Had it succeeded, the elections would have failed and perhaps given Ukraine's opponents further pretense for mischief, aggression, and de-stabilizing activities. While the Ukrainian Government was able to fight off the attack, what became clear was the vulnerability of Ukraine's IT systems. Ukraine needs help in replacing its IT infrastructure and in protecting it going forward.

MOVING UKRAINE FORWARD

There are also some hopeful signs for Ukraine as it moves forward from these elections. The losers in the Presidential election conceded honorably and in ways that can foster unity. President-elect Poroshenko has already taken significant steps to move the country forward. He has indicated that he will retain the current Prime Minister (Arseniy Yatsenyuk) and others in the current government. He has stated his top priorities are to maintain the unity of the country by reaching out to eastern regions, tackling corruption, and creating jobs.

President-elect Poroshenko has also indicated that his government will undertake important constitutional reforms. A strong democracy relies on a constitutional order that protects citizens' rights, as well as limits government authority and provides for the rule of law.

In particular, the new government has expressed its willingness to consider amending the constitution with the goal of decentralizing and subsequently granting greater power to regional and local councils. The direct election of governors, which would certainly result in greater decentralization, is one of the changes under consideration.

The West can and should play a supportive role in facilitating changes in local governance. North American and European expertise can be brought to bear in providing experience and technical assistance in a way that can assist in producing local governments that are more accountable to the needs of the Ukrainian people. Similarly, the West can play a critical role in advising Poroshenko and his government on innovative and effective means to show real results in the battle against corruption, which continues to be one of the key concerns of voters, and is also detrimental to Ukraine's hopes for greater foreign investment.

Ukrainians stand united in their desire to remain a unified country. In IRI's April 2014 public opinion survey, the vast majority of Ukrainians (90 percent), even those in the east, want their country to remain united. In addition, a majority of Ukrainians (54 percent) want Ukraine to join the European Union. Ukrainians deserve a leader who will undertake these issues immediately.

DEVELOPING A LONG-TERM STRATEGY TO ASSIST UKRAINE

At this critical juncture in Ukraine's further democratic development, it is essential that Ukraine's friends support the Ukrainian Government and civil society efforts to build a prosperous and democratic country. In supporting these efforts, the United States, through mechanisms such as the United States Agency for International Development, should increase democratic assistance to the country to provide support to the newly elected government to enact reforms. There is a great need to accelerate government capacity-building to fight corruption and build citizen-oriented structures. This will build citizen faith in leaders and harness the energy of the Maidan. To further promote the development of a diverse and representative party system in Ukraine, additional assistance should be provided for the development of political parties (particularly new and emerging ones resulting from the Maidan movement). In addition, Ukraine's friends must seek to enhance the capacity of a burgeoning civil society in Ukraine, which rediscovered its voice during the Maidan movement. Marginalized groups, such as youth and minority groups like the Crimean Tatars, need to be supported in their efforts to develop a democratic and unified Ukraine.

Finally, the U.S. and others should support the building of linkages between Ukrainians from eastern, southern, central, and western parts of the country. Ukrainians want to learn from each other and strengthen relationships with their fellow Ukrainians from different parts of the country. They also want to acquire the knowledge and skills to be able to build a democratic and prosperous country. IRI stands ready to work on these and other great initiatives that can help the Ukrainian people.

CONCLUSION

Mr. Chairman, recent events in Ukraine make clear both the challenges and possibilities that lie in the months and years ahead for the Ukrainian people. The fact that Ukrainians, in the span of a few short months, were able to remove from office a corrupt but powerful leader and then just weeks later, conduct national elections that met international standards, is remarkable. The fact that all of this was accomplished in the face of threats and violence sponsored by one of the world's most powerful governments is historic. It will take every bit of this same resolve, and more, to meet the daunting economic, security and governance challenges. At IRI, we believe there are many things the U.S. can and should offer to help.

The Ukrainians, not their friends in the West, are responsible for shaping the country's future. They have a unique history and rich culture all their own, and they want to chart a path that meets their own needs and aspirations, not anyone else's. As one of IRI's Ukrainian staff proudly stated recently, ''We went to the Maidan to find Europe, and instead we found Ukraine.''

The CHAIRMAN. Mr. Wollack.

STATEMENT OF KENNETH WOLLACK, PRESIDENT, NATIONAL DEMOCRATIC INSTITUTE, WASHINGTON, DC

Mr. WOLLACK. Mr. Chairman, Senator Corker, members of the committee, thank you for this opportunity to comment on recent developments in Ukraine.

With support from USAID, as well as the National Endowment for Democracy, and the Department of State, and the Governments of Sweden and Canada, NDI has conducted democracy assistance programs in Ukraine for the past two decades. Most recently, we fielded an international observer delegation for the election, which was led by NDI Chairman Madeleine Albright and former Spanish Foreign Minister Ana Palacio. And we were also fortunate to have Jane Harman as part of the leadership of that delegation.

Ukraine has turned a corner onto a decidedly democratic path. At the same time, the country is facing an extraordinary set of challenges, some new and some long-standing. Most pressing is the external threat from Russia, which has illegally occupied Crimea. Russian-backed and armed separatist operations in the eastern oblasts of Donetsk and Luhansk amount to an undeclared war against Ukrainian sovereignty.

On the domestic front, the challenges are no less daunting. The economy is in crisis. Corruption, by all measures, has been rampant, and public confidence in political institutions is low. While there has been overwhelming support in both the east and the west of the country for Ukrainian unity, there are divisions over the distribution of governmental powers. External forces are working to exploit and politicize these divisions through a campaign of disinformation.

The Euromaidan demonstrations were sparked by anger over the Yanukovych government's abrupt refusal to sign a European Union treaty. But they were sustained for 3 months by a more basic demand for dignity. They introduced accountability to citizens as a requirement of governance. However, the redistribution of power from elites to citizens will be sustainable only if civic and political leaders find post-Maidan ways to keep people engaged in politics. The country now has the opportunity to translate the energy of this watershed moment into a sustainable democratic trajectory, one that makes future Maidans hopefully unnecessary.

The first test of Ukraine's ability to navigate this transition was the May 25 Presidential election, and by every measure, Ukraine passed that test.

This was perhaps the most important election in Ukraine's independent history. Where they were allowed to cast ballots in the vast majority of the country, Ukrainian voices came through loud and clear. They voted for sovereignty and democracy, and they did so not with celebratory fanfare but with sober determination. In observing elections in more than 60 countries, including previous polls in Ukraine, rarely has NDI heard such positive commentary about the process from political contestants and nonpartisan monitors alike.

After President-elect Poroshenko's inauguration this weekend, the government will need to pursue open and consultative governance practices that incorporate the interests of Ukrainians from all regions of the country. He and other leaders will need to focus as much on process as on policy outcomes. Delivering on citizens' expectations will be impossible without encouraging meaningful public participation. Beyond the urgent need for economic reforms and the diversification of trade and energy supplies, these expectations include constitutional changes, including decentralization; serious anticorruption measures, the number one priority for Ukrainians throughout the country; and judicial reform.

Since February, the Government and the Parliament have enacted an impressive set of reforms and civil society organizations are helping to shape an ambitious agenda. I draw your attention to the Reanimation Package of Reforms, an impressive civil society initiative to improve election laws, procurement practices, education policy, and access to public information among other issues. By listening to and consulting with citizens and communicating in clear terms how short-term sacrifices will lead to longer term improvements, government leaders can help smooth the path to results.

For political parties, the challenge will be to build support from the grassroots up and base policies and strategies on citizens' concerns. This will require parties to embrace new ways of organizing.

The Euromaidan movement showed that citizens can wield considerable political power. But by their very nature, street protests are inchoate. Sustained popular participation requires leadership and structures. Channeling the energy of Euromaidan into the day-to-day and admittedly less exciting business of reform and governance is the next hurdle. These efforts need to be disseminated more widely throughout the country.

It will be important for the national dialogue on ensuring rights and representation for all Ukrainians to accelerate and deepen. This process, which is now underway, would benefit from broader and more active participation from civil society.

The impact of past U.S. assistance to Ukraine is more visible now than ever before. Years of corrupt and inept governance masked much of Ukraine's promise. But that sustained support from the United States, nonetheless, helped democratic groups get established, expand, accumulate skills, and survive through political hardships. Also in the new political environment, partners of U.S. assistance projects can be found among the most active reformers in the Government, Parliament, political parties, and civil society.

Ukraine now needs help in all of its priority reform areas. Ukrainian political and civic leaders have been unanimous in requesting such support. There are major financial needs to be sure. In addition, Ukrainians are eager for technical assistance, peer-to-peer contacts, and linkages to international counterparts. Just as Ukraine's problems will not be solved overnight, international engagement needs to expand and aim for the long term.

Thank you very much.

[The prepared statement of Mr. Wollack follows:]

PREPARED STATEMENT OF KENNETH WOLLACK

Mr. Chairman and members of the committee, thank you for this opportunity to comment on recent political developments in Ukraine in the wake of the May 25 Presidential election.

NDI IN UKRAINE

With support from USAID, as well as the National Endowment for Democracy, the Department of State, and the Governments of Sweden and Canada, NDI has conducted democracy assistance programs in Ukraine for the past 25 years. These efforts have focused on strengthening citizen engagement in issue advocacy, governance, political parties and elections, and on women's participation in politics.

Most recently, NDI fielded an international election observation mission that was led by NDI Chairman Madeleine Albright and former Spanish Foreign Minister Ana Palacio. Delegation leaders also included Wilson Center President Jane Harman, former Hungarian Member of Parliament Matyas Eorsi, and former U.S. Senator Ted Kaufman. The mission's leadership reflected the importance of a trans-Atlantic commitment to a democratic and sovereign Ukraine. NDI also helped Opora, Ukraine's largest nonpartisan citizen monitoring group, deploy 2,000 observers across the country, including to Donetsk and Luhansk, and conduct a parallel vote tabulation that confirmed the official election results. Along with several European groups, NDI also supported 350 observers from the European Network of Election Monitoring Organizations (ENEMO), a coalition of the leading citizen monitoring groups in Eastern Europe and Eurasia.

EXTERNAL AND INTERNAL CHALLENGES

Ukraine has turned a corner onto a decidedly democratic path. At the same time, the country is facing an extraordinary set of challenges, some new and some long-standing. Most pressing is the external threat from Russia, which has illegally occupied Crimea and massed troops on Ukraine's eastern borders. Russian-backed and armed separatist operations in the eastern oblasts of Donetsk and Luhansk amount to an undeclared war against Ukrainian sovereignty. This represents an urgent threat to Ukraine's territorial integrity as well as a challenge to the European security order.

On the domestic front, the challenges are no less daunting. The economy is in crisis; corruption, by all measures, has been rampant; public confidence in political institutions is low; and citizen patience is limited. While there has been overwhelming support in both the East and the West of the country for Ukrainian unity, there are divisions over governmental structures. While these would not in themselves threaten the integrity of Ukraine, external forces are working to exploit and politicize these divisions through a campaign of disinformation.

EUROMAIDAN AND ELECTIONS

The Euromaidan movement and the Presidential election have set a solid foundation for Ukraine to address many of its long-standing internal challenges. Euromaidan set the stage for the election. The election has in turn set the stage for further and deeper reforms.

Euromaidan was sparked by anger over the government's abrupt refusal to sign a European Union treaty, but it was sustained for 3 months by a more basic demand for dignity and respect from government. The Euromaidan demonstrations that began last November fundamentally altered the political dynamics in the country. They highlighted Ukrainians' demands for change, including more transparent, accountable and uncorrupted political practices as well as respect for basic civil and political rights. They led to the collapse of a government, its replacement by a more reform-oriented and EU-focused interim government, and the scheduling of a snap Presidential election. Less visibly, they introduced accountability to citizens as a requirement of governance for perhaps the first time in Ukraine's history.

Euromaidan drew participants from across the country and spawned similar demonstrations in cities in all regions, reflecting widespread consensus on these issues. Public opinion research also demonstrates that Ukrainians across regions share a desire for national unity, more responsive governance and greater public integrity.

Tragically, the Euromaidan demonstrations resulted in the deaths of more than 100 Ukrainians and injuries to many more. Other deaths in the east and south, including those in a fire in Odessa, present the need for a concerted reconciliation process.

However, the redistribution of power from elites to citizens prompted by Euromaidan will be sustainable only if civic and political leaders find post-Maidan ways to keep people engaged in politics. Street protests are blunt instruments for governing and cannot be prolonged indefinitely. The country now has the opportunity to translate the energy of this watershed moment into a sustainable democratic trajectory—one that makes future Maidans unnecessary. It remains to be seen how effective this transition to more conventional forms of participation will be.

The first test of Ukraine's ability to navigate this transition was the May 25 Presidential election. By every measure, Ukraine passed that test.

This was the most important election in Ukraine's independent history. The NDI observer delegation listened to the people of Ukraine in meeting halls, government offices, and polling places. Their voices came through loud and clear. They voted for sovereignty and they did so with determination. They wanted the world to know that Ukraine could not be intimidated by external threats. They achieved their purpose.

By turning out to vote across the vast majority of the country, Ukrainians did more than elect a new President. They showed the world their commitment to unity and democracy. Their votes conveyed that these principles should be valued over geopolitical strategy or leaders' personal enrichment. Ukraine's electoral administrators, campaigns, government authorities, election monitors and voters showed courage and resolve in fulfilling their responsibilities in compliance with Ukraine's laws and international democratic election standards. The losing candidates deserve commendation for their constructive responses to the results. In observing elections in more than 60 countries since 1986, including previous polls in Ukraine, rarely has NDI heard such positive commentary about the process from political contestants and nonpartisan monitors alike.

In most of the country, the elections were generally run well and proceeded without major incidents. Voter turnout was 60 percent. The preelection period and Presidential election were virtually free of formal candidate complaints. Polling station commissioners cooperated to facilitate voting and address issues, while large numbers of nonpartisan citizen observers and party poll watchers, including many women, witnessed the proceedings. Across the country, voters often stood in long lines, waiting patiently to cast their votes.

Isolated problems did crop up. Molotov cocktails were thrown overnight at some polling stations, but those precincts opened in the morning for voting. On election day, bomb threats temporarily closed some stations, but the security forces responded effectively and voting resumed. Observers also noted incidents of overcrowding at polling sites, police presence inside polling stations, late arrival of mobile ballot boxes, and poor accessibility for voters with disabilities. None of these concerns, however, diminished confidence in the process or the results.

By contrast, in Crimea, Donetsk, and Luhansk, representing just under 20 percent of the electorate, most voters were denied the opportunity to vote.

No polling took place in Crimea due to the Russian occupation. Crimea is home to 1.5 million registered voters, representing 5 percent of the Ukrainian electorate. The Central Election Commission (CEC) reported that approximately 6,000 Crimean residents registered to vote in other parts of the country, which was the only procedure available to them.

In Donetsk and Luhansk, two of five Eastern provinces, armed groups carried out illegal actions—including seizures of government buildings and electoral facilities, abductions and killings of journalists and widespread intimidation—aimed at preventing the elections. Even in the face of such violations of fundamental rights, electoral officials opened 23 percent of polling stations in those two oblasts. International and Ukrainian election observers witnessed these officials' brave and determined efforts. Ultimately, only small percentages of eligible voters in Donetsk and Luhansk were able to cast votes.

Any disenfranchisement of voters is regrettable. Universal and equal suffrage for eligible citizens is fundamental to democratic elections. However, the three cases of Crimea, Donetsk, and Luhansk should not negate the fact that the vast majority of the electorate—more than 80 percent—had the opportunity to cast ballots for the candidate of their choice.

Also, it is important to note the source of voter disenfranchisement. In most countries where NDI has observed elections, disenfranchisement has been caused by authorities or political contestants interfering with the process for electoral advantage. In Crimea, Donetsk, and Luhansk, the responsibility lies with foreign forces occupying Ukrainian territory and armed groups seeking to prevent voting, despite good faith efforts by election officials. Such disenfranchisement cannot be allowed to negate the legitimacy of elections or the mandate they provide. Unfortunately, disenfranchisement occurred in parts of Afghanistan, Pakistan, and Georgia in recent elections due to terrorism by nonstate actors or foreign occupation. Nevertheless, those actions did not negate the credibility of the overall process.

All NDI observers commented that the mood surrounding the election was marked less by celebratory fanfare than by sober determination, reflecting both a recognition of the challenges that lie ahead and a resolve to meet them.

NEXT STEPS

The Euromaidan movement made change possible and the election added momentum. The task ahead is to make such change sustainable. After he is inaugurated this weekend, President Poroshenko will need to pursue open and consultative governing practices that incorporate the interests of Ukrainians from all regions of the country. He and other leaders will need to communicate effectively the prospect of short-term sacrifices and deliver on the longer term expectations of the Euromaidan movement. Moreover, they will need to focus as much on process as on policy outcomes. Delivering on citizens' high and varied expectations will be impossible without opening channels of communication and encouraging meaningful public participation.

These expectations include:
* Improved security;
* Constitutional reform, including decentralization and outreach to the east and south;
* Economic growth and stability;
* Anticorruption measures;
* Diversification of trade and energy supplies;
* Political institutions that channel dissent, facilitate debate and respond effectively to citizens' concerns;
* Transparency, integrity, and accountability in all aspects of public life;
* An open and fair judicial process; and
* A legislative process that is based on consultation and open debate.

While some of these expectations were articulated on the Maidan, public opinion research has shown that they are shared by all Ukrainians, including those who did not participate in the demonstrations and even those who opposed them. In public opinion polls, Ukrainians consistently cite corruption as their top concern. Some meaningful reforms have already been undertaken; many more are needed for Ukraine to reach its democratic potential.

For many years, political parties, civil society organizations and government agencies were isolated from one another and from citizens. However, the building blocks for a more unified and inclusive system are now in place. The Rada and the current Cabinet of Ministers represent all regions. President Poroshenko was elected with pluralities in all oblasts that voted, gaining an inclusive and strong public mandate.

Since February, the Government and the Parliament have enacted an impressive set of reforms. Civil society organizations are holding politicians accountable and helping to shape an ambitious agenda. I draw your attention to the "Reanimation Package of Reforms," an impressive civil society initiative to improve election laws, procurement practices, education policy, and access to public information, among other issues, through civic advocacy and strategic cooperation with parliamentary and government allies. It is an important example of a successful transition from "the square" to sustainable political participation.

The task ahead is for parties, civil society organizations and government to become citizen-centric, rather than leader- or oligarch-centric. Giving citizens meaningful influence over these political institutions would contribute to their coherence and effectiveness.

Government: The government and the parliament are under intense pressure to deliver results to an impatient public. Ukrainians have historically had limited trust in politicians and parties. One way to address this challenge would be to focus on public consultation along with meaningful reforms. By listening to and consulting with citizens—and communicating in clear terms how short-term sacrifices will lead to longer term improvements—government leaders would help smooth the path to results.

Political Parties: Ukraine's political parties need to rebuild. Former President Yanukovych's Party of Regions is on the wane. Other established parties performed below expectations in the elections. Even the President-elect's party is small. A coherent and loyal opposition to the government has not yet formed. In the past, the leading political parties have been top-heavy and personality-driven. Those structures are now struggling to survive in the changed political environment. However, it is promising to see that some new parties are emerging. These groups seem well positioned to infuse established parties with new energy or gain traction in their own right. For all parties, the challenge will be to build support from the "grassroots" up and base policies and strategies on citizens' concerns—including demands for transparency and public integrity. This will require parties to embrace new ways of organizing that are more labor-intensive but ultimately more sustainable. Local and parliamentary elections, which could be called as early as this fall, will present opportunities for building a genuine multiparty system.

Civil Society: Ukrainian civil society is robust and Euromaidan has only added to its vitality. The Euromaidan movement showed that determined, organized citizens can wield considerable political power. By their very nature, however, street protests are inchoate. Sustained popular participation requires leadership and structure. Channeling the energy of Euromaidan into the day-to-day and admittedly less-exciting business of reform and governance is the next hurdle. Initiatives like the "Reanimation Package of Reforms" and, before that, nonpartisan citizen election monitoring projects and campaigns to defend freedom of assembly and other rights set great examples of effective organizing. These tactics need to be disseminated more widely throughout Ukraine so protesting is no longer the advocacy strategy of first resort.

It will be important for the national dialogue on ensuring rights and representation for all Ukrainians to accelerate and deepen. Indeed, this process, which is now underway, would benefit from broader and more active participation from civil society.

The added benefit to resolving these internal crises is that doing so puts Ukraine in a stronger position to address the external threats to its sovereignty and territorial integrity. The tangible benefits of democratic governance and closer ties with Europe and the West will ultimately eclipse hollow propaganda to the contrary.

INTERNATIONAL ASSISTANCE

The impact of past U.S. development assistance to Ukraine is more visible now than ever before. Years of corrupt and inept governance masked much of Ukraine's promise. But that sustained support from the U.S. nonetheless helped democratic groups to get established, expand, accumulate skills and survive through political hardships. Nonpartisan citizen election monitors introduced transparency to Ukraine's electoral procedures. Initiatives like the Chesno Movement promoted accountability among candidates for public office. Civic coalitions like "For Peaceful Protest," a long-time advocate for the right to freedom of assembly, helped to organize Euromaidan around the principles of peacefulness and voluntarism. Also, in the new political environment, partners of U.S. assistance projects can be found among the most active reformers in the Government, Parliament, political parties, and civil society.

Ukraine now needs help in all of its priority reform areas. In NDI's meetings throughout the country over the past 3 months, Ukrainian leaders have been unanimous in requesting such support. There are major financial needs, to be sure. In addition, Ukrainians are eager for technical assistance, peer-to-peer contacts and linkages to international counterparts—in the areas of constitutional reform and decentralization, civil service reform, procurement, public integrity, judicial reform, communications, citizen outreach and engagement, transparency and accountability, and political party and civil society strengthening. Just as Ukraine's problems will not be solved overnight, international engagement needs to aim for the long term.

The CHAIRMAN. Well, thank you all for your testimony.

And before I start a round of questioning, let me recognize that Ukrainian Ambassador Motsuk is here, and we welcome you, Mr. Ambassador, to this hearing.

The G7 statement says we stand ready to intensify targeted sanctions and to consider additional significant restrictive measures to impose further costs on Russia, should events so require. As I listened to what I think was a majority of you, it would seem to me that the collective view here—and correct me if I am wrong—is that that time is already here. Am I wrong in what I have heard, or is that basically what you are saying?

Ambassador JEFFREY. Yes, the time is here, Senator.

Ambassador PIFER. Yes. The Russians, I think, are thoroughly involved in what is going on in eastern Ukraine, and they have the power to stop that if they wished.

Ms. HARMAN. And, yes, our asymmetric strength against Russia is our economic power. Their economy, even before the individual sanctions, was in bad shape, and it has gotten worse. And by doing this quickly, although it will be some short-term pain for Europe in particular, it will be medium- and long-term gain for Europe and for us. We have an energy sector, obviously, that could export substantial amounts of energy to Europe.

Ambassador GREEN. Mr. Chairman, the position of Western leaders previously was that if Russia interfered in the conduct of the elections, that more sanctions would be coming. I think it is clear that they did, in fact, take a number of steps to interfere with those elections. So I would argue that the time has come, most definitely.

The CHAIRMAN. You mentioned a cyber attack. How do we know that to be the case, that it emanated from Russia?

Ambassador GREEN. That was actually brought to us by our Ambassador, by the U.S. Ambassador in Kiev, and has been reported, although not as widely reported, quite frankly, as I think it deserves.

But while they were able to fight it off, it laid bare what a number of people have been suggesting, and that is that so much of the infrastructure system, which was operated by Russian-supported government officials, has been infiltrated and is weakened, and that seems a basic way in which it happened.

The CHAIRMAN. And, obviously, if they had been successful, they could have undermined the veracity of the election and therefore pursued their goal. So your point is well taken.

Let me ask you this. What do you think, from your experiences, will affect Putin's calculus? I know what his calculus is. At least I think I know what his calculus is. What is going to affect his calculus in a way that changes Russia's course of events under his leadership?

Ambassador PIFER. I would argue that the possibility of more intense Western sanctions could—and I say could, not necessarily will—affect his calculus. If you look at what is happening to the Russian economy, it was already in difficulty in 2013, but the sanctions and the threat of more robust sanctions have increased the problems for the Russian economy. And many Russian economists go back and say that Vladimir Putin has this implicit social compact with the Russian people in which he says you are not going to have much in the way of political freedom, but in return, you are going to get economic security, a growing economy, and high living standards. And Mr. Putin delivered spectacularly on that between 2000 and 2008. Last year, some Russian economists were saying tht even the projected growth in 2014 of 2 percent would not be enough for Mr. Putin to hold up his end of the bargain. So we need to try to increase that pressure.

Now, I should say one of my colleagues at Brookings, who is very knowledgeable about Russia—his concern is that what will happen is that it may play a different way, that Mr. Putin may seize on the sanctions and then use them as the excuse, blame the West for the economic difficulties, and then use that to sidestep his own economic mismanagement. But I would argue, that even if there is just the prospect of changing his calculus in the way that makes him change the policy, the West should do it because of the egregious nature of Russian actions in the last couple of months.

Ms. HARMAN. And let me add to that. As we know in American politics, it is the economy, stupid. And the polling in Russia right now shows nationalism running high, but over time, as sanctions bite further—and I do think there should be some sectoral sanctions done very carefully. I agree with Ambassador Pifer that they need to be done carefully—people in Russia will have a lower standard of living. And let us understand that Putin already has not learned Colin Powell's Pottery Barn rule: if you break it, you own it. He now owns Crimea or at least temporarily is renting Crimea. And he is stuck with a horrible economy and the need, which he has had to fulfill, to increase the pensions and the payments for state workers in Crimea, and that is another hit on the Russian budget.

I think Senator McCain is right when he says Russia's economy is a gas station and Russia is a gas station posing as a country. And if that gas is turned off, at least with respect to Europe, that is a huge hit. He has made a deal with China, but I think that shows desperation. That does not show long-term advantage.

The CHAIRMAN. Ambassador Jeffrey.

Ambassador JEFFREY. I would like to add that I am very much in favor of sanctions, and I think we have seen particularly some secondary effects of them. We should continue and strengthen them, trying to keep the Europeans on board because they will take most of the pain.

Nonetheless, I am a little bit concerned if we think that, to sum it up briefly, 21st century values, economic development, people power and such triumphs over aggression, over nationalism, and over 18th and 19th century values. I am not sure in the parts of the world where I have been deployed that that is true, and I really do not think that is true with Mr. Putin certainly, because he is very clear in his goals, or with the Russian people. His desire—and it seems to have a lot of support—is to recreate something like the old Russian imperial power as one of the great powers with a droit de regard over much of the area around Russia today stretching into Eurasia and into Central Europe. This is a very dangerous strategy.

You asked how can we respond against it. He is facing the EU and the United States with a $2 trillion economy. We have $30 trillion. We have six times the population, two or three times the number of forces under arms and far better equipped.

Why is he doing this? And why is he seemingly having some success? Because we are divided. We are not sure what the threat is, and in particular, we are reluctant—the United States to some degree and the Europeans even more—to meet force with force. That is why it is so important to take military moves while also strengthening the economic and the political sanctions and strictures against him because he does not believe we are going to stand up for our values.

The CHAIRMAN. So you would be supportive of the President's billion dollar initiative on the security and NATO?

Ambassador JEFFREY. Absolutely, except it should not be contingent upon action. He has the authority. He has the equipment. He has the troops to start doing this tomorrow.

The CHAIRMAN. Ken.

Mr. WOLLACK. I would just like to make one point about Russia's role in the election. We should not lose sight of the fact that 17 percent of the electorate was disenfranchised either because of the occupation of Crimea or the Russian-backed separatists in Donetsk and Luhansk.

The question remains with the fighting still going on in these two oblasts where the Russian goal is to make Ukraine ungovernable. So the actions to try to destabilize the country before, during, and after the elections continues.

The CHAIRMAN. I have a lot of questions, but I am only going to say one final question. Then I am going to turn to Senator Corker.

What can Poroshenko do in eastern Ukraine? Some of you have talked about decentralization of government. I would like to hear exactly what you think that means because, of course, the Russians wanted a federated system so they could pick Ukraine apart. I assume you do not mean that. Protections for the use of the Russian language; or inclusion of more easterners in the government? Do some of you have thoughts as to what Poroshenko can do to try to consolidate the eastern part of Ukraine as part of the national body politic?

Ms. HARMAN. We do not want to dominate this at this end of the table. But I listed five things, and I think the border with Russia is absolutely crucial. From all of the information that I have seen on the public record, there are truckloads of people who may or may not be Russian but they are coming over the Russian border, and they are mostly, we think, Cossacks, Chechens, or Russian nationals. So closing that border to that kind of traffic is absolutely critical. The Ukrainians probably do not have the capacity to do that. Obviously, the Russians do. And I think having an international call on them specifically to do that right now would at least expose the role that they are playing. And I think we are all united in understanding what that role is.

It is tragic that some Ukrainians who wanted to vote were prevented from doing that, as Ken Wollack just said. I thought it was 13 percent, but he says 17 percent of the country could not vote. And then there are, of course, the folks in Crimea which we all view as an occupied part of Ukraine, most of whom could not vote either.

Ambassador PIFER. Mr. Chairman, I would make the comment that I think Mr. Poroshenko has said that he wants to make his first trip as President to Donetsk, and he may well find a receptive audience there. It is important to bear in mind the majority population in eastern Ukraine is ethnic Ukrainian. They may use Russian as their first language, but they are ethnic Ukrainian. And polls showed some very interesting things in the last several months. The polls show that, while many people in eastern Ukraine were uncomfortable with what happened in terms of the change of power in Kiev at the end of February and that they regarded the acting government as illegitimate; 70 percent wanted to stay in Ukraine. They did not want separation. They did not want to join Russia. Large majorities criticized, condemned the armed seizures of the buildings by the separatists. They did not want to see the Russian army come. So I think there is audience there that he can appeal to.

I think decentralization of power, to some extent, not as far as Russia would like to go, makes sense because the Ukrainian Government right now is overly centralized. So, for example, making regional governors elected as opposed to appointed by the President would be a positive step. Pushing some budget authority out to the regions would be a positive step in terms of more efficient, effective, and accountable governance.

Also, Mr. Poroshenko has said that there would be some status for the Russian language. This seems to be a very touchy issue in eastern Ukraine, and there are things I think that he can do that would, in fact, begin to make the majority of that population in eastern Ukraine feel more comfortable that Kiev is looking out for its political and economic interests and undercut the support for the separatists that are being backed by Russia.

The CHAIRMAN. Ambassador Green, last word.

Ambassador GREEN. Mr. Chairman, first off, with respect to the polling, IRI has done a great deal of polling. And Ambassador Pifer is precisely right. Every part of the country, even the area in the far east which may have wanted more autonomy from Kiev, wanted to be part of Ukraine, viewed themselves as Ukrainian, did not see discrimination, and very much wanted to remain part of Ukraine.

I would argue that what the President-elect needs to do is to take a look at what Putin did in the lead-up to this election. Putin sought to sow seeds of doubt to destabilize, sent agents in, shut down radio stations, and so on and so forth. So what I think Mr. Poroshenko will need to do, among other things, is to build a media that can communicate non-Moscow messages, give an accurate picture, provide channels for Ukrainians from all parts of the country to get together in social media platforms, to communicate with each other and exchange ideas.

Finally, I would argue that a significant exchange program which creates east-west, north-south understanding inside the country to build a new generation of leaders that think of themselves entirely as Ukrainians and not regionally, I think, is vitally important. Again, based upon what we have seen from President Putin, that is very much what he fears.

The CHAIRMAN. Senator Corker.

Senator CORKER. Thank you, Mr. Chairman.

I think it is good to note that we have people on both sides of the aisle here that are pretty uniform in their thinking about both Ukraine and Russia, and that is good to hear. And I think we have a lot of that on our committee.

So it seems to me it is very evident to all that we have a country that has underperformed, has missed 20 years, if you will, of development and has huge challenges within the country. Then you have this other issue that is of major geopolitical significance to the world. They come together at Ukraine on the border. They affect much of our policy over the last 60 or 70 years that Europe would be whole, democratic, and free. So we have two really big issues, and if Ukraine does move to the West, it also creates internal issues to Russia as Russian people see a country evolving in a very different direction from where they are and that certainly poses a threat to their leadership there.

So let me just start. The newly elected leadership is impressive. He is an oligarch, I agree, Congressman Harman. At the same time, it was not a state-owned enterprise. He did sort of make it the, I will not say the honest way, but a different way than a lot of the oligarchs.

Is there any difference of opinion that he is absolutely committed to making the transition that is necessary to be made within the country? Does anybody feel like that is not the case?

Ms. HARMAN. I hope he is committed. We have to see what he does. We thought Yushenko was committed. We thought Yushenko was the new leadership for Ukraine, and he turned out to be enormously disappointing. Some people thought that Yulia Tymoshenko was the new voice of leadership, and she turned out to be very disappointing. So I think it really matters what he does.

Senator Corker, I just had maybe one suggestion for the way you framed this. I think that Ukraine is Ukraine. Ukraine is not part of Europe. It is not part of Russia. It is a country that is situated next to NATO countries. Many people in Ukraine are very interested in, and have a long history of, connecting to Europe, but some people in Ukraine are also very interested in, and have a long history of, connecting to Russia. And I think the best outcome for Ukraine is to have a somewhat decentralized government where Ukraine can be both and certainly latched to Europe. That is in our interest, but I also think it is in Ukraine's interest. But if Russia would only back off, if we could get this to change, I do not think it would be bad for Ukraine also to choose, if it chooses, to have robust ties to Russia.

Senator CORKER. And it is very apparent that that is what the newly elected president plans to do.

Did you want to say something, Mark?

Ambassador GREEN. I was going to say I was one of those who had the chance to meet with Mr. Poroshenko the day before the election, and while I absolutely agree the proof is in the pudding, he was impressive in laying out a clear agenda for what needed to be done, including constitutional reform and taking on corruption. So he certainly knows what to do. Obviously, I believe that we should be there when requested to try to help him get there.

Mr. WOLLACK. I think in our meetings with the President-elect and with the Prime Minister, I think everybody understands the challenges that lie ahead, and I think they are all deeply committed to these issues. And they realize that now there is a second chance for meaningful reforms in the country.

At the same time, I think we have to put our faith in institutions and processes as well and not just individuals. And the parliament is going to play an important role. Civil society is going to play an important role, and the question is whether all these various sectors of society can work constructively together in order to achieve the goals that we all share.

Senator CORKER. Well, I too was impressed. And I think Yatsenyuk is very impressive, and hopefully a team will be put together to move things ahead.

Since I am running out of time, I will stop here, but I was going to ask, is there anything that you see the Western countries that are involved and care about Ukraine not doing other than, I know you mentioned some military equipment and training that needs to take place, that should be done now? I know it has to be Ukraine itself that makes this happen. I could not agree more. But, obviously, assistance from us is going to be needed and persistence is going to be needed. Is there anything that you see right now? Just if one person could respond very briefly because I want to move on to something else. Is there anything that you see that is missing right now in the complement of efforts that would be helpful to help them move along? Yes, sir.

Mr. WOLLACK. I would just mention two quick things.

Number one, I think the commitments on financial assistance should not be caught up in bureaucratic hurdles here, that funds have to flow in a timely way.

And second, as my chairman talks about, when Madeleine Albright talks about, the Marshall Plan was not only about funding. It was also about massive technical assistance. And when we met with the government there, they welcomed large-scale infusion of human resources in the country on all the major reform issues. They look to the United States for expertise. They look to the diaspora community for expertise. They look to the Europeans, particularly Poland, for those expertise. Poland is engaged on the constitutional reform issues as well. I think on civil service reform, on all of these issues, having technical assistance on a large scale embedded in ministries and government offices, in civil society—this is all welcome. They believe this international engagement is critical at this time.

Senator CORKER. So, Mr. Jeffrey, I want to move on to the other topic, and that is Russia. I had an executive in my office this morning. I will not name the name or the company. I do not think he would like that to occur. But you have this issue you just mentioned. This is a major geopolitical issue, the biggest that has happened since 9/11. And yet, the tools that we are willing to use obviously are very different than the tools we used in 9/11. I agree, especially having just come from Poland, Romania, and Estonia, this is a major geopolitical event. And how we respond to this is going to reverberate for generations.

And so you mentioned sanctions, and many of us here have pushed for more robust sanctions. Some people would say—this executive would say—that we pushed for globalization around the world to try to create democracy because we think that our way of doing business causes the world to be better place. I agree with that. At the same time companies all have become intertwined. They all work through joint ventures. And I could not agree more.

I would like to see sectoral sanctions. I think we have already crossed the redline, and sanctions ought to be in place for what happened in eastern Ukraine.

But how do you respond to the folks who come in who, I have to say, do not have an impact on me in that way, but how do you respond to people who say what you just said, and how do you respond to the President when he talks about how we do not want ourselves to be split from Europe? We want to go with them. Is that an appropriate place to be, or should we be even more forward than where we are today?

Ambassador JEFFREY. In my view, you have to stay pretty closely synced with Europe, but we do seem to have, in many respects, an unusually robust ally in Angela Merkel compared to where the rest of the Germans and where much of Europe is. And so we can nudge her forward, and there has been some success.

Senator CORKER. Do you really see that?

Ambassador JEFFREY. I would say that compared to her population, she is tougher than most Germans. The overwhelming majority of the German population basically on every poll or most polls shows understanding for Putin, and this is what we have to deal with.

In terms of the economic issues, it is not a question of cutting Russia out of the global economy. We cannot do that. They are not Iran. And that is basically not our argument with them. The problem is they are able to use blackmailing political leverage based upon some of their economic activities, most notably selling gas to Europe, and secondarily, the way that Russian funds are deposited. I spent almost an hour with Putin in 2007 where he harped on this theme in a very unpleasant conversation with President Bush. And they see this as political weapons.

So what you need to do is to diversify in the best market economy tradition, for example, European gas purchases. And I know that that is in the draft bill. But there are other seemingly minor things that are so important. The European Union is looking to take on the monopolistic aspects of the vertically integrated Russian gas industry from production to transportation, to actually marketing in many countries, and to break that up. Those are the kind of things that will not only send a signal but will eventually rob Russia of its somewhat strange capability to blackmail an entity, Europe, that is many times larger an economy and power in every sense.

Senator CORKER. So I know my time is up, and hopefully you can respond to someone else, Mr. Green, in just a minute.

I want to say I think the biggest fear that I have was expressed by someone in Poland last week, and that is that we end up accepting a bitter peace with Russia. In other words, yes, this is the biggest geopolitical event since 9/11, but we are not willing to use the same tools. So we end up in a situation where they exude extremely bad behavior. We do not do much. And we end up in this bitter peace where we have this nation that has broken international norms and laws, reneged on agreements, and in order to keep peace, we continue to go along in this bitter peace that, in essence, creates a lot of insecurity in Eastern Europe and causes people to question the United States.

So with that, I know other people have questions. Mr. Chairman, thank you.

The CHAIRMAN. Senator Cardin.

Senator CARDIN. Mr. Chairman, thank you very much, and let me thank all of our witnesses for their extraordinary work.

I want to thank NDI and IRI for their participation in the monitoring of the Ukrainian elections under the auspices generally of the OSCE. Senator Portman and I were there on the ground, had a chance to visit polling stations, and had a chance to meet with the leadership of the country. So we share your observations, and I thank you very much. We very much have similar observations.

Mr. Jeffrey, I want to just concur in your overall concern that the international order of dealing with these types of incursions is very much at jeopardy here, and it goes well beyond Ukraine. Clearly, what Russia did in Crimea, what they are doing in eastern Ukraine violates international commitments and agreements, et cetera, and we can go through all of them, including the OSCE core commitments.

But it is also now being looked at in the China seas. I went from Ukraine to Vietnam, and all I heard in Vietnam is their concern about China in the South China Sea. When I was in Japan, I heard about the concerns about the East China Sea. If we do not engage a better order, we are going to see what happened in Ukraine used by major powers elsewhere to solve territorial disagreements.

So I just want to come on very strongly in support of your comments that we need to get NATO involved in Ukraine because it does involve the security of our NATO alliance, and we need to have an enforceable code of conduct in the China seas so that we can restore some semblance of discipline in how we deal with territorial disputes.

I just really also wanted to underscore points that have been made of what we need to do in Ukraine. Congresswoman Harman, I agree with you completely that the message of protesters in the Maidan was much more fundamental than just taking sides on ethnic disputes. They want a country that responds to the needs of their people, and they want a country free from corruption. And that is not going to be easy in Ukraine. It is going to take a long-term commitment to get the country to perform at the level that the protesters expect and will demand.

So, therefore, first and foremost are our economic programs to help them so that they have a performing economy, and I think we all agree on that.

We also need to work internationally. The point that was raised about bringing Europe along with our policies is absolutely essential. And I really do think President Obama deserves great credit for being able to mobilize Europe in a more cohesive fashion than we have seen in previous problems in other places of Europe.

But it does require attention to the economics and the fundamental economics, which deal also with energy. And we very much need to be aggressive in providing short-term and long-term alternatives to Ukraine on their energy issues.

It also involves sanctions, Mr. Chairman. I think there is total agreement here that we need to be tougher on sanctions and that sanctions work and that the threat of sanctions has worked. But the threat only works to a certain degree if you do not deliver. Russia's actions during the election and the words that were given beforehand I think indicate that it is time for us to move forward with additional sanctions. They have to be strategic, and they have to be well thought out, and they have to be in coordination with Europe.

But I want to get to another point that has been just talked about, and that is whether we can affect the balance on the border between Ukraine and Russia. Right now, as you pointed out Congresswoman Harman, the people from Russia who want to come into Ukraine have no difficulty getting through that border. And, yes, it would be nice if President Putin would do something about it, and I think we have to be very firm about that. But President Putin does not do what he says. So I do not want to take his word that he will maintain the border as being safe for Ukraine against incursions from Russians.

So I think we have a responsibility to help build up the border security for Ukraine. I think the United States and Europe can play a pretty constructive role in strengthening the border security issues. OSCE has capacity here although the Russians may make it difficult for OSCE to give that type of technical support. But it seems to me that we can find an effective way to help Ukraine deal with its own defense of its border. And I just would like to get your view as to whether that would be a priority, should be a priority, and whether that can effectively be carried out.

Ms. HARMAN. Well, you know I agree with you. How to do it does matter. What the process is does matter. It needs to be a Ukrainian response, it seems to me, but inviting in international organizations to help is right. The OSCE has an interesting position in the country. OSCE convened roundtables, three of them, led by Wolfgang Issinger, former German Ambassador to the United States, who by the way now is a scholar at the Wilson Center. We are very proud of him. And those roundtables began to achieve something that Mark Green is talking about, which is a conversation in the country to unite all the parts of the country. A really good idea. And they are going to continue.

But OSCE is interesting because it is a member organization that includes Russia. And I was there in Vienna following my trip to Ukraine and was told that the way the procedures work at

OSCE, Russia is kind of locked in for a 6-month period to the actions OSCE is taking in Ukraine. So it seems to me it would be really smart to get OSCE mobilized to do exactly what you are talking about with help from NATO to increase the——

Senator CARDIN. The mission is in Ukraine. It has been there.

Ms. HARMAN. Right.

Senator CARDIN. We do have capacity.

Ms. HARMAN. And it is in east Ukraine, and to mobilize more resources at the border. And then see. Putin responds to strength. Let us see him push against that, an organization that he is a member of that is just asking for reasonable border controls. Big trucks full of armed people, who may or may not be Russian, who are destabilizing the country should be stopped.

Senator CARDIN. They are going to need technical assistance. They are going to need equipment. They are going to need more than the international community is currently providing.

Ms. HARMAN. I would say, yes, surely. I mean, Ukraine has a very undercapitalized defense system.

But I would just end with our strength against Russia is our economic strength. I think that is where we can stop Russia more effectively, and I think sanctions are by far our best weapon. We always talk about the terrorists attacking us asymmetrically where we are weak. Where Russia is weak is its economy, and sectoral sanctions, that I think everybody here supports, done intelligently and quickly could get a very rapid response.

Senator CARDIN. I am for that, but I would not trust Russia to stop the flow into Ukraine. They need border security.

Ambassador PIFER. Senator, if I could just add. I agree we can do more to assist the Ukrainians in terms of tightening their border. But I think particularly in the short term it is going to be difficult given the length of the border between Russia, Donetsk, and Luhansk. And my guess is as long as the Russians are determined to get things across that border, they will find ways. So in the short term, the pressure of additional sanctions on Russia—we have got to get Russia to be part of the solution, not part of the problem.

Ambassador GREEN. If I can add, let us also remember the history of brush fire battles. We also need to help the Ukrainian Government in that part of the country deliver. We need to help them build their capacity, build their IT infrastructure, help them deliver basic services, and really provide the links to the government that those communities are looking for that have been taken apart by the destabilization activities. Mr. Putin comes in, knocks out the radio stations and attempts to sponsor these separatist movements. Success in building governing capacity should also be part of the solution. I do agree on the hard force side, but it is also important, I think, to create that sense of linkages to the national government and the kinds of successes that reinforce for all those communities why they want to be Ukrainian in the first place.

Ambassador JEFFREY. Senator, I agree with everything my colleagues have said, but at the end of the day, what you have laid out is a military problem and it is not a military problem that we are ignorant of because we saw this in Vietnam. We saw it in Iraq. We see it today in Afghanistan where you have an insurgency supported and in this case largely generated from across the border. It is a tricky problem, as we have seen in those other places, but there are ways to deal with this.

First of all, all of the things stated to strengthen the Ukrainian Government, to strengthen the support of the people, to strengthen the economy. That then leverages into a counterinsurgency strategy of stabilization that puts a minimum on force, although force is necessary, and a maximum on reconciliation and slowly moving in, picking the low-hanging fruit, as you do in any properly organized stability operation, so that the area controlled by the pro-Russians does not expand.

Meanwhile, at the same time, you are putting a lot of pressure through sanctions, through diplomatic activities, through strengthening NATO, which is something Putin does not like, watching American ground troops on his western borders, to send a signal that it is just going to get worse if you keep this up. And what are you gaining? Bit by bit, Ukraine is deepening its sovereignty. It is deepening its stability. And in the long run, you are not going to win this insurgency. And then there can be a time to move this forward. So you need the political. You need the economic steps. You need to reach out to the population. But it is also a military activity.

Mr. WOLLACK. Senator, could I just comment on what you said regarding the impact of Ukraine and other places? Moldova will be signing the association agreement later this month. It will be holding parliamentary elections in November. And I think we have to have a very watchful eye on what is happening in Transnistria, what will happen following the signing of the association agreement in a very small and very vulnerable country close by.

The CHAIRMAN. Senator Johnson.

Senator JOHNSON. Thank you, Mr. Chairman.

Mr. Jeffrey, you just used a business term, which I like, a low-hanging fruit, which implies prioritization.

My colleagues, certainly on the Republican side, realize that I really try and address any problem with a strategic planning process. What I would like to do is quickly go through something like that. The strategic planning process starts with describing reality. You cannot deny it. You have to bow to reality and then, based on that reality, set yourself achievable goals. So I want to just kind of lay out my assumptions what the reality is and I want to get your reaction, particularly if you are disagreeing with me in terms of where I am going wrong.

The first assumption. It makes no economic sense to Russia what Vladimir Putin is doing. There is no economic sense.

Number two, as a result, this is all about Putin's ego. This is all about his ability to maintain control and power.

Number three, what gives him power is his oil and gas, you know, the gas station, and his monopoly control over supply which is quite honestly crazy. In business, customers should be in control, not the supplier.

Here is another reality. We can talk about sanctions. I have a somewhat contrary view to that. Most of the harm to the Russian economy occurred before any sanctions were imposed because the world does recognize what he is doing makes no economic sense and it is scaring investors. So Vladimir Putin has done his own economic harm, and that will continue regardless of what the West does. And by the way, another reality is because sanctions are a double-edge sword, mutually harmful, I do not believe the West will ever have the will to impose the kind of sanctions that will affect his calculus whatsoever. So we can talk about them. I do not believe they are going to be imposed. And by the way, this may be not a bad thing. I would rather inflict one-sided pain on Vladimir Putin, make him pay a price without us having to pay a price.

So that is, to me, the assumption that this is the reality situation.

From that, now you establish goals. To me the number one short-term goal—and I think it is obvious—is Ukraine must gain control over the east. Anybody disagree with that? Okay.

We need to help them. Right? So we can talk about sanctions. They will not get imposed. So we will not be changing Putin's calculus, but we can help them secure the east. So we need to do those things. That is number one.

Number two. We certainly, when we were on the ground, heard about the incredible effect of the propaganda coming from Russia. We need to counter that aggressively. We can do that too. Can we not?

So those are the two, from my standpoint, top priority short-term goals.

Then medium-term. I think this is really what was so hopeful about the protest in Maidan is that really was the coming together of the Ukrainian people after 20 years to say, okay, we are sick of the corruption. So we need to do everything in terms of our actions. If we have to tie aid or help to make sure that anticorruption laws are passed, I think we should do that. That is the medium term. Another part of the solution is we have to have a successful government in Ukraine.

Then long-term. Again, understanding what gives Vladimir Putin power is his oil and gas monopolies. We need to break that up. So we should be taking actions today to make sure that Vladimir Putin understands that his monopoly will not be in place, not 2, 3, or 4 years from now.

So again, that is just my way of thinking. Here are the assumptions. Here is the reality, and I think you have to bow to it. And here are the goals that we can actually achieve and we can help.

Where am I wrong? What am I missing? I will start with you, Congresswoman Harman.

Ms. HARMAN. Well, I generally agree. None of us mentioned Russian television, but Madeleine Albright who, as I mentioned, headed the NDI delegation of which I was a member, speaks Russian. And she kept talking about the domination of this message from Russian TV into Ukraine everywhere that she went. And we do not, and the Ukrainians do not, have an effective counter. So I commend you for putting that on the table. I think it is a very important short-term goal.

We have discussed the border. I think everyone agrees that more needs to be done on the border.

In the medium term, my understanding is that there are now, as part of this package of laws that Ken Wollack mentioned, the Reanimation Package, or at least what has been passed to date, some strong anticorruption—there is an strong anticorruption law. The problem is it is not enforced. And that should be a huge early step of the Poroshenko government, and hopefully that happens.

On the long term, absolutely break up the gas monopoly. I still am hoping for sectoral sanctions. But we have an opportunity in this country—Tom Friedman, the op-ed writer for the New York Times, has called it a grand bargain—to get everyone to buy into a package of safe development of energy, safe transportation of energy, and then export of energy, a variety of energy, not just LNG, to replace Russia as the gas station for Europe.

And there is another point. Senator Markey I think was going to be here. But I know he has a notion that we should help Ukraine—perfect. I think we rehearsed this. [Laughter.]

Hello to my former colleague.

Senator JOHNSON. If you are going to talk renewable energy, again I would think that would rank pretty low on the priority scale.

Ms. HARMAN. Well, but let me make the point.

Senator JOHNSON. Because, again, we have to take a look at what is going to be most effective.

Ms. HARMAN. All right. Speaking for Senator Markey, which I have done for many years——

[Laughter.]

Ms. HARMAN [continuing]. His point is that Ukraine is the least efficient user of energy of any of the countries in that region.

Senator JOHNSON. They have their windows open in the wintertime because it gets so hot.

Ms. HARMAN. If we could help promote energy efficiency in Ukraine, we would reduce Ukraine's dependence on Russia. So there are steps like that that we should be taking.

Senator JOHNSON. Ambassador Pifer.

Ambassador PIFER. Senator, I agree with most of your construct. I would make just two points. One, I do think that there is value in sanctions because otherwise——

Senator JOHNSON. Let me ask you. Do you honestly think they are going to be imposed to the point where they would actually have an—again, if we could actually impose them, I think it might affect Vladimir Putin's calculus at a cost to the West. So, again, because of that cost to the West, do you honestly think they are going to be imposed? Because like Congressman Green said, Vladimir Putin has crossed the line. He has done what we said if he did we would impose them, and we have not imposed them yet.

Ambassador PIFER. No, I agree.

I can see sanctions that I think would have a serious impact on Russia. I cannot tell you politically that I am sure we could bring the Europeans to do that.

Senator JOHNSON. That is a real problem. So, again, I am just trying to think what is achievable, what is possible. Let us do what is possible.

Ambassador PIFER. But I think there is still a possibility. So I think we should still be trying to push because otherwise the egregious nature of what has happened—I mean, this is the first time since 1945 where a big country has used military force to take territory from a small country in Europe. There needs to be some penalty for this.

The other point on the gas question. I think we should be doing things, including looking at exporting American LNG, to begin to make it more difficult for Gazprom. But I think we do have to be realistic. Europe now gets about 30 percent of its gas from Russia. Europe will only very slowly wean itself away, and we should be finding ways to encourage that.

I would also agree with what Jane Harman said about working with Ukraine. Ukraine has huge possibilities if they get more efficient use of their energy to reduce their gas consumption. Plus, they also have this possibility, perhaps in 5 to 7 years' time, to produce huge quantities of unconventional gas within Ukraine. And if the Ukrainians make that happen, they could actually be in a situation where by 2020, they perhaps could, with the combination of domestic production and importing gas not from Russia, but from the West, be in position where they would not need any gas from Russia. And that would be a very important change in this dynamic that now exists because Ukraine's biggest economic vulnerability to Russia now is the fact that it depends on Russia for about 60 percent of its natural gas.

The CHAIRMAN. Senator Kaine.

Senator KAINE. Thank you, Mr. Chairman.

I would like to continue on this line on energy because we have had a number of discussions on this committee. While there are some sharp disagreements on the committee about things like LNG exports, I think there are also some strong agreements, whether it is helping reverse flows of energy back to Ukraine from some of its western or northern neighbors working with Ukraine to develop its own energy capacity. Algeria is interested in more exports of energy under the Mediterranean to Europe.

My sense of the Russian economy is it is a rust belt economy with natural resources, and the toughest thing that we could do for them is to do just exactly what Senator Johnson said and kind of break up that monopoly. So we ought to be looking at all of those opportunities even including potential resources like Algeria that would like to ship more energy to Europe. So it is not just what we can do, although we can do a lot, but other partners who would want to help them wean away from that monopoly is critical.

I wanted to ask just about one topic and that is the polling about the east, the Donetsk and the eastern area. You talked about that earlier, Ambassador Green. The polling is pretty strong that huge numbers in the east do not want to be part of Russia. They do not want to be severed from Ukraine. But the polling is also pretty strong that they have a great distrust of the Government in Kiev, and some of that has been because of the propaganda campaign from Russia. But some of it was also because of steps like this kind of effort to potentially strip away Russian as an official language in a population that, though Ukrainian ethnic, speaks Russian as a first language.

Obviously, this is something that the President needs to address immediately. You have talked about this effort by the President to say I want to go to Donetsk first. But maybe in a little more granular detail, talk about the kinds of things you think the President needs to do right out of the gate to start winning over eastern Ukrainians to the notion that Kiev will not be stiff-arming us but will be including us and respecting our traditions, including the Russian language.

Ambassador GREEN. Well, you have just laid out some of it yourself. I do think it is important. Symbols are important and so are the early steps from Poroshenko in going to the east. But it is also, again, capacity building so that the government is seen as being able to deliver on some of the basic needs and wants in that area.

I also would not separate out what we have all been talking about in terms of corruption. One of the reasons why some of the far reaches of the country are so angry with Kiev is because the economy was plundered by the previous President, all rife with corruption. In many ways, that is what the Maidan movement was about. Sure, there were events that sparked it in terms of backing out of the movement towards the EU, but it was also this basic anger toward a government that was riddled with corruption, unable to deliver and unable to provide for basic services.

Couple that with linking that part of the country to Kiev in terms of a national dialogue through the media, exchanges that create a youth network of reform-minded Ukrainians, those may seem like long-term activities. I would argue they are not. I would argue they are immediate steps that need to be taken. I think each one of those steps would send very important signals to that part of the country in addition to all of the other things that we have been talking about.

So in terms of what members of the committee have been putting forward, my own view is all of the above. If we are looking for simple solutions, I am not sure they are there. I think we need to take a very comprehensive approach that has both the security aspects to it, to the capacity building, to the basic infrastructure that is necessary for delivering services, for creating a sense of purpose and unity in having that dialogue.

Senator KAINE. Ambassador Pifer and then Mr. Wollack.

Ambassador PIFER. Thank you, Senator.

Let me give you maybe six pieces of a package that could be used to overcome the divisions within Ukraine.

First of all, the government would offer to deescalate its use of force if the armed separatists laid down their weapons, left the occupied buildings.

Second, this idea of decentralization, which Mr. Poroshenko has already talked about, pushing some authority out to the regions and to local levels.

Senator KAINE. Election of governors rather than appointment.

Ambassador PIFER. Exactly, yes.

Third would be early Rada elections. The big news about the May 25 election was it lifted part of that cloud of illegitimacy over the acting government because you now have somebody who has a strong democratic mandate. Early elections for the Parliament would give the Parliament also a renewed democratic legitimacy, and that would be important.

Part number four would be agreement—and again, Poroshenko has talked about this. Some validation, some affirmation of official status to the Russian language is a very big issue in eastern Ukraine.

A fifth element would be a very strong and a very visible anticorruption campaign. Tens of thousands of people were on the streets there. It was in part about the fact that they are just tired of corruption that permeates every level of society.

And I think another part would be his foreign policy approach. You have already had people—Mr. Poroshenko, the acting government—state they do not want to get too close to NATO. Six years ago, I testified that Ukraine was ready for a membership action plan, which they were. I have since come to the conclusion that NATO is just a very controversial topic within Ukraine, and there may be some way for the Ukrainians to say without saying ''never'' but to say ''not now'' in a way that I think would be useful in avoiding what could be otherwise a very controversial topic.

Senator KAINE. How confrontational or provocative is a continued move toward the EU association in eastern Ukraine? So, for example, there has been a political agreement, but economic pacts are supposed to be signed in June. Is that provocative in eastern Ukraine?

Ambassador PIFER. It is certainly less provocative. Particularly among the young in eastern Ukraine, I think that they look to the idea of Europe and see that is where they want to go. So while maybe not pushing NATO, I think Ukraine should go ahead and go forward with the association agreement with the European Union.

Now, the problem that they have is what I believe triggered the Russian activity from Crimea's seizure on to what you see going on in eastern Ukraine is that the Russians do not want to see Ukraine do that association agreement because Ukraine moving in that direction becomes irretrievable for Moscow.

Senator KAINE. So it does not provoke eastern Ukrainians but it may be additionally provocative to Russia.

Ambassador PIFER. Exactly.

Senator KAINE. I only have 30 seconds. I want to ask one very fast question.

One concern that I had early was the presence of the ultranationalist parties in Ukraine and what power they might have, parties that have some strong anti-Semitic tendencies. I viewed it as a real positive that their candidates of the two main ultranationalist parties got less than like 2.2 percent of the combined vote in the presidential election. Am I right to read that as a really positive trend?

Ms. HARMAN. I think it is a very positive trend. They got clobbered. But I also think we have to allow free expression in the country. I abhor those views, but I think if we try to censor and bury those views, we are doing Egypt.

I just would add one more thing to Steve's list, and that is possible amnesty for those in east Ukraine as part of a bigger deal. And I would caution against early Rada elections because there has to be enough political capacity for all of the new voices to be able to run campaigns. We saw that in Egypt again. The elections were too early and they could not win.

Mr. WOLLACK. I would just add one thing too in this. I think the Russian actions in Crimea, Donetsk, and Luhansk has had the unintended and opposite effect in a majority of provinces in the eastern and southern part of the country. There is much more eagerness on their part—and the elections showed it—for Ukrainian unity as a result of those actions. So I think it has had a huge impact.

I would just also add on the national dialogue, to expand and deepen the national dialogue would be something that the President could do as well.

The CHAIRMAN. Senator Flake.

Senator FLAKE. Thank you.

It is good to see some of you I have not seen in a while. I apologize for missing the oral testimony. But a couple of issues, and I apologize if you have covered them.

How do you believe, Ms. Harman, the Russia-China deal on natural gas affects the ability for us to export LNG in an effective way? Part of the attraction here is, although it would take a while to get the infrastructure in place for it to make a real difference, price signals would have been sent immediately. To what extent is that nullified by this big Russia-China deal?

Ms. HARMAN. Well, I said earlier that I see it as a sign of desperation. I think Russia was beginning to believe—and I still believe it should be a reality—that we, the United States and Europe, are going to cut off their ability to sell gas to Europe. So they desperately wanted another market. We do not know, or at least I do not know, what the terms are of that deal. Many people speculate they are not very favorable to Russia. And until we know that, I am not sure we can fully answer the question.

But I think there is an enormous opportunity for the U.S. energy industry to get its act together, to work with the Europeans, and to find new markets in the medium term, including the export of LNG. I understand that there are regional markets that price LNG, and we do not want to lose the enormous cost advantage that we have here in America. On the other hand, I think we need to be a little more strategic, and if there are international opportunities for us to sell energy, not just LNG, to Europe, we should fully explore those.

Senator FLAKE. Thank you.

With regard to sanctions, as we mentioned, Russia has already tripped some of the measures. They have passed the threshold where we said that we would move forward with additional sanctions. The Europeans are not following.

What in your view, Mr. Jeffrey, will it take for the Europeans to come on board?

Ambassador JEFFREY. First of all, overt Russian military action by conventional forces I think is the redline that would push the Europeans to take a very dramatic step forward. I do not think that Putin is going to do this. I think that is why he stood down some of his forces, while he is now using irregular forces rather than his own elite spetsnaz types as he used in Crimea.

Nonetheless—and this gets back to Senator Cardin's question earlier—even the sort of kiddy sanctions that we are seeing and long-term gas and oil and other energy decisions that we are discussing here have, as you mentioned, Senator Flake, tremendous future implications for the movement of money and economic decisions around an integrated world. And it is hurting Russia in many ways when we are taking these steps, even if they are not bold or major, even if they are not like what we did against Iran or, as was earlier said, we do not use the tools we used after 9/11. Well, we went into Iraq. We are not going to go into Russia that way. But even these minor steps have very significant consequences.

And the other thing is they are hard for us and particularly the Europeans to do. Putin does not think that we will do hard things. Every time we do a hard or halfway hard thing, we are sending a signal to him that who knows what we are going to do tomorrow if he keeps this up. And that is a good thing.

Senator FLAKE. Ambassador Green, when our delegation was there just before the seizure of Crimea, the acting Prime Minister said, with regard to the Ukrainian military, we have nothing that shoots, runs, or flies I believe, or something like that. They will develop some of that capacity over time.

But what are the political implications of using military force in the east? How is it played and how will it play in the future in terms of the dynamics with the Russian speakers and the leanings of some people? What are the military implications of action by the Ukrainian Government in the east?

Ambassador GREEN. Well, first off, we have been talking about, throughout this hearing, it is essential that the Ukrainian Government show that it is able to govern and actually to deliver. Obviously, a huge part of government's purpose is to be able to deliver security along its borders. So I think that is terrifically important.

What you point to is that the infrastructure, security infrastructure, military and IT, has been weakened. It has been weakened and is currently no match for Russians whether they——

Senator FLAKE. That goes across the military, police force, across the board.

Ambassador GREEN. One of the things that we heard quietly from Ukrainians is that we are worried that the Russians know exactly what we are going to do before we do it because they are the ones who helped set up this IT infrastructure in the first place. In terms of what the West can do, the West can help, can respond to requests, and help the Ukrainians build their capacity on all levels to be able to secure the borders but also to deliver the basic services that link those communities in those areas to a central government.

Right now, with all the propaganda that they are getting from Moscow, with the armed thugs who are going back and forth and destabilizing wherever they can and starting problems like tossing Molotov cocktails into polling places, it raises doubts in the minds of the communities along those borders. My own view is that we need to help them assuage those doubts. I think a big piece of it is basic capacity building so that there is some semblance of governing authority.

If I can return to something that you said in your remarks, which I think is key, we have a tendency in the West to think that signals and symbols are only long-term, and I could not disagree more. I think what you are talking about is so important because sending signals of Western support, Western dedication and devotion to not just Ukraine but to the entire region is essential because in those communities that have historically weaker links to central governments, where they are being bombarded with all of these mixed signals, I think it is important that they know that the community of democracies is there and will be there. So I think it is a long-term signal that has an immediate payoff. It is terrifically important strategically.

Senator FLAKE. Thank you all.

Thank you, Mr. Chairman.

The CHAIRMAN. Senator Murphy.

Senator MURPHY. Thank you very much, Mr. Chairman. I really appreciate the discussion that we are having on what our next path should be on sanctions. Having spent the last several months in pretty close consultations with our European allies color me fairly pessimistic that they are ready to take the next step. We have referenced in previous hearings the small dinner that some of us attended with Chancellor Merkel in which she can charitably be described as stuck in her current position regarding robust caution on sanctions.

Some European nations are not sitting still. They are actually moving the other way.

Senator Johnson and I, amongst others, sent a letter to the French today asking them to halt their sale of two Mistral-class warships to the Russians, the very type of warships that were actually used in the invasion of Crimea.

So I want to just pin the five of you down on your exact recommendation for us on sanctions because I think we have got a good conversation about this. But assuming that the Europeans are not willing to move with us on the next level of sanctions and to use Ambassador Jeffrey's analogy, a move from kiddy sanctions to tiger sanctions, sectoral sanctions—assuming that they are not ready, would you recommend that the United States precipitously move forward unilaterally with sectoral-based sanctions regardless of whether the Europeans are ready to join us? And if you can give just quick answers, and if you have a caveat, add it. That would be fine.

Ms. HARMAN. Well, it is nice to see all my former colleagues on the Energy and Commerce Committee in the House.

I do not think that unilateral sanctions work well. We have seen this movie in Iran. I think put maximum pressure on Europe and hope that Angela Merkel can be helpful to do this. It is in their interests to do this. It will be cheaper in the long run to do this. But if Europe will not go along, I would move to larger individual sanctions because getting at some more of these folks does get at the energy sector. A lot of them are major players in the energy sector in Russia, and it does hurt. And I think the sanctions that have been imposed to date, not fully effective, have had a big bite on Russia.

Senator MURPHY. If people can give quick answers to this question. I have one more after this.

Ambassador PIFER. I think we need to push and see if we can do sanctions in concert with Europe, but if Europe will not go along, I would agree, more individual sanctions. I would also target families. There are ways to keep people who want to travel to New York and Miami, for example, from coming here.

I guess the one area I would look at, if we decide to go unilateral, would be in the financial area just because so much of the international commerce is denominated in dollars. This would require somebody smarter than me about these questions, but maybe looking at sanctioning one major Russian bank like Sberbank or Gazprombank. Could the United States do that itself? I think that would have significant implications on the Russian economy, and I think we could have some effect. We would have to calculate what blowback there might be against the U.S. economy.

Ambassador JEFFREY. Unilateral sanctions if we cannot get concerted ones with the Europeans, but we do have to be careful. They should be designed to persuade not provoke the Europeans because maintaining solidarity with these guys is still very important.

Ambassador GREEN. I would agree with what you have just heard. Not speaking for IRI here, speaking only for myself, I think one of the least reported stories in recent months is what has been happening in Moscow and the fact that Putin has taken a number of steps to impose restrictions on his own people and to shut down dialogue, which means he obviously fears the effects of sanctions.

My own view is that as you have heard here, ratcheting up individual sanctions and family sanctions are important signals, and I think we should constantly be pushing our European allies and remind them of the lines that have already been crossed in an effort to try to get broader sectoral sanctions.

Mr. WOLLACK. NDI does not take a position on sanctions.

But I would just make the point that I think the Ukrainians and I think the international community sees Crimea as lost at least for the short term. And I do not think we can afford to see de facto occupation in two of the five provinces in eastern Ukraine. And whatever can be done to hold Russia accountable for what is taking place in Donetsk and Luhansk I think will be very, very important.

Senator MURPHY. Here is my second question. We may have time for one or two people to answer. But it is a much broader question about the future of NATO and the future of article 5 protections. I agree with you that Europe will certainly react if there is a movement of troops across the border, and the idea is that they are protected under the mutual defense covenant in NATO. But Russia is perfecting a new form of warfare in which they do not march troops across the border, in which they very slowly but methodically contest areas, gain control of areas with a range of tactics from intimidation to bribery to provocations to little green men with no Russian uniforms. And so this is a longer term challenge for us.

But is article 5 still a sufficient protection for countries along Russia's border?

Ambassador JEFFREY. Yes, it is, Senator Murphy, as long as it is backed with a real capability. That is why it is so important that the President has put U.S. light infantry along those borders, and I hope through this billion dollar program it will be heavier forces and reinforced with NATO.

To be sure, the light green men were facilitated by the presence of 40,000 traditional motorized rifle and tank regiments along the border that basically like scissors, paper, rock blocked the Ukrainians from taking more effective military action in the early days against Crimea. So he has got a very sophisticated set of military and paramilitary steps. The first capability that the eastern states of NATO need is a stronger military with U.S. forces there as we had in Berlin and other places so they know it only may be a few Americans today but there will be many more tomorrow.

Senator MURPHY. Jane, let me just ask a slightly different version of the question to you. Let us say the tactics that are being used in eastern Ukraine were used in Romania or Bulgaria. Let us say Russia was actively funding separatist movements within those nations. My impression is that does not trigger article 5, but should we be having a discussion about whether that protection is sufficient?

Ms. HARMAN. I think we should have a discussion about how to meet our NATO obligations. Article 5 is central to that. I also think the other NATO members have to put more into the fight both in terms of resources and money.

And a final point on sanctions which I forgot. A senior Russian official was recently at the Wilson Center and suggested that we yank the visas for Russian Duma members to go to the south of France and Florida. They all have their dachas there and they love their vacations more than they love their political jobs. And that would really get their attention, and I think that is something that Europe could go along with even if the restaurants in the south of France lose a little money.

Ambassador PIFER. Senator, if I could just add briefly. I think it would be actually very useful within NATO for a conversation to be about the appearance of little green men. What happens if 150, quote, local protesters seize a television station in eastern Estonia? I think NATO ought to have that discussion in advance so then when it happens, NATO has an answer ready. My worry is that if it happens, it is not going to be useful if NATO debates for 4 or 5 weeks whether that is an article 5 contingency.

Senator MURPHY. That is my point.

Thank you, Mr. Chairman.

The CHAIRMAN. Senator Shaheen.

Senator SHAHEEN. Thank you all very much for being here.

And I would like to pursue that line of questioning a little bit because it is my understanding that over the next few weeks the NATO Defense Ministers are working to develop a readiness action plan. And I just wonder if you all could talk a little bit about the kinds of things they ought to be thinking about, not just with respect to Ukraine, but with respect to some of the other countries in Eastern Europe that are potential targets for this kind of Russian activity and what kind of response we ought to be thinking about from NATO. Should we have a more assertive position, either rhetorically or in terms of other symbolic actions, that we could be taking now that would help send a very strong signal both to Russia about taking further action but also to our allies about our support for them?

So I do not know who. If you would like to speak to that first, Mr. Pifer?

Ambassador PIFER. Going back to 1997, NATO has tried to be nonprovocative in terms of its military deployments on the territory of the countries that joined from 1999 on. So there have not been permanent United States deployments in places like Poland or Romania or the Baltic States. I think what we have seen in the last 3 months, the Russians have fundamentally changed the rules. And so now it is time to consider something—I think the Pentagon uses the term ''persistent,'' but moving toward some kind of a permanent American military presence in the Baltic states and Poland. I do not think that these have to be large units. I do not think they have to have significant offensive capability. They are basically there as a trip wire, but that trip wire worked and kept Berlin free for 35 years.

The one thing I would add, though, that does bother me a bit. And I have tried to talk to my European friends about this, that when you look at the on-the-ground permanent deployment now in the three Baltic States and Poland, you have one American airborne company with about 150 troops in each of those places. It should not just be American. What I have been trying to lobby for is it would be great if you could have four European countries, have a German company paired with the American company in Lithuania, a British company with the American company in Poland and so on. I think that would be very good in two ways, one in terms of sending a signal to Moscow that the article 5 commitment is shared by all NATO allies. And I think it would also probably send a good signal to Capitol Hill where at some point you may be getting asked questions about why is this just an American burden.

Senator SHAHEEN. Well, I certainly agree with that. I wonder if any of you are willing to speculate on why they have been so reluctant to do that. Is it because of the concerns about the relationship with Russia and their trading opportunities and their dependence on energy, or is there something else going on?

Ambassador JEFFREY. First of all, there is the 1997 agreement, and if you look at the language of it, it is clear, as Ambassador Pifer said. The conditions—and it said explicitly under the current and foreseeable conditions, we will not be making large, permanent deployments. Well, it is clear that, God, if the conditions have not changed under what we have seen in the last few months, they will never change. And secondly, we are not even talking about, as Steve said, large and permanent. We are talking about a few companies from various countries falling in on what we would call battalion packages with the other four companies on alert ready to be flown in almost immediately and fall in on their equipment. That can very rapidly—I saw it in Kuwait in 1998. That can very rapidly generate 5,000 troops. The Berlin brigade was a trip wire, but as you remember from those pictures of Checkpoint Charlie in 1962, it was a trip wire with M–60 main battle tanks.

If you have a conventional military capability, again you block the ability of Putin to intimidate the reaction to the infiltration, the little green men, little seizures of things along the borders because people can deal with those as police problems without having to worry about 10,000 Russian troops coming across the border.

Senator SHAHEEN. I think that is worth exploring a little more, but I want to change the subject. I am sorry. I had another hearing, so I was not able to get here to hear your testimony.

But I wanted to explore the economic situation in Ukraine because I know early in this crisis, one of the overwhelming views that we heard was that if Ukraine's economy does not improve, that it creates a situation where the whole country could fall. Again, I do not know who wants to address this, but if you could speak to where we are in terms of economic assistance for Ukraine, to what extent do we think that that is having an impact there. Is there more we should be doing? Are we seeing the austerity measures that are being called for having a negative effect in a way that is challenging? And then corruption. Are we seeing any potential positive efforts to address corruption in a way that we think will have long-term effects?

Ms. HARMAN. Well, I think we have all said more or less the same thing, but I think I am the only mother and grandmother on this panel. And we need tough love here. Everyone cares about Ukraine's economic future, but Ukraine has to care about Ukraine's economic future. And the anticorruption piece is absolutely huge. If the resources from the West just go into McMansions for a few oligarchs or fat bank accounts, wherever, that is unacceptable. And we have already seen that. So the Poroshenko government, which starts Saturday, has to move out smartly, and he says that he will do that. That is point one.

Number two, there will be austerity measures required to qualify for IMF loans, substantial, huge IMF loans. Other countries like Egypt are not prepared to do this. There is a huge political cost to this. When you tell somebody your gas bill is going to go up by 100 percent or more, et cetera, that is hard to hear. But this is the time. This is the third chance for Ukraine for this government to say to folks, hey, you fought and died in the Maidan. You want a different kind of government. This is what it will take, and after we do this for a short period of time, the aid will come and we will build a noncorrupt country with a sensible jobs program and your future will look brighter.

Ambassador PIFER. If I could just add. Right now, Ukraine has an offer in the next 2 years from the IMF, other international financial institutions and western donors between $25 billion and $35 billion. So there is a good sum of money out there.

The other bit of good news. My understanding is that when the IMF team went to Ukraine in March to talk about the program, they said for the first time in dealing with Ukraine in 20 years, the Ukrainians said here is the problem, here is our to-do list. Every other time, the IMF said here is your to-do list. This time, the Ukrainians had the right to-do list. So they know technically what they have to do, and they understand that their ability to access that $25 billion to $35 billion will be tied to their continued implementation of reforms.

I agree with Jane. I think the big question is can they sustain the political support for those austerity measures. On May 1, as one of their prior actions for the IMF, they raised the price of heating. May 1 is a great time to raise the price of heating because no one needs it, but in November–December when people see their bills up 60–70 percent, that is when the government is going to have to come out and say we just have to grit and get through this the next couple of years because this is key to unlocking the economic potential.

Senator SHAHEEN. Mr. Chairman, my time is up, but I know Mr. Green wanted to comment on that.

Ambassador GREEN. Senator, thank you.

IRI has been polling in Ukraine for a long time, and we have conducted two polls right before the election, as well as, of course, the polls themselves in the election. I think the good news is the Ukrainian people have their eyes open. They understand the path ahead is not going to be an easy one. The polling shows that they are prepared for tough measures and difficult steps. The polling also shows that the leash may be a short one.

So my own judgment is as long as the government sends clear signals that it is moving to take on corruption, there is some hope that they will take on these aggravating factors. Then they have got a mandate. Then they have got the capacity to take these challenges on. The Ukrainian people are well educated. Ukrainian people know what they are up against. The Maidan is very much still front and center to them and close to their hearts and those who tragically were killed in the Maidan. So there is a sense of euphoria tempered by realism and as long as they start making those very clear steps, I think the mandate is there.

Senator SHAHEEN. Thank you all very much.

The CHAIRMAN. Senator Markey.

Senator MARKEY. Thank you, Mr. Chairman, very much.

There is an old saying that if you give a person a fish, you feed him for a day. If you teach him how to fish, you feed him for a lifetime. So that is what we are really talking about here.

Ukraine is the second least energy efficient country in the world, second from the bottom. Ukraine, if it just improved not to Germany's level, but just to Poland's level, would back out almost all of the natural gas it imports. Teach a country to fish.

It has vast untapped natural gas resources. Vast. Third in Europe. Teach a country to fish, to develop its own energy resources. That is where we should be. That would scare Russia. That would petrify Russia. That would be the Ukrainian people banding together themselves, saying we must do this.

So I introduced a bill this morning to deal with this Achilles heel of Ukraine, which doubles the funding for the State Department, USAID, Export-Import Bank, OPIC, and U.S. Trade and Development Agency to deal with this issue both of energy efficiency and natural gas development inside their own country, to leverage programs that are already there, but to bring in our expertise to help them to telescope the timeframe that it takes for them to do it. So that is, without question, where we have to be as a nation. That is our opportunity.

And exporting LNG from our country—that might heat their homes for a day. We can do that. But that is really not where we should be.

And I will just add parenthetically here for those who are criticizing President Obama's plan on Monday that the EPA announced to reduce our greenhouse gases, and who are decrying the increase in electricity rates here in America for doing that are the very same Republicans who are also supporting exporting our natural gas, which is going to so dramatically increase our own domestic electricity rates that it will dwarf any increase that comes from the President's announcement on Monday about what the EPA is doing. It is not even close, if that is a concern.

But back to this subject, which we should be able to work together on on a bipartisan basis, that is where we should be, and that is what we should be leveraging.

You are an expert on this, Congresswoman. Can you talk a little bit about energy efficiency, about this whole area, and how dramatic a difference you believe it can make, given your own experience with your lighting legislation here in America. You really do know this issue cold.

Ms. HARMAN. Thank you, Senator Markey. It is kind of interesting to see you at the bottom of the queue on the committee. This is a new for me.

Senator MARKEY. A little bit of humility is a good thing.

Ms. HARMAN. You are very humble now.

Senator MARKEY. I am proud of my humility.

Ms. HARMAN. You and I worked closely together on energy efficiency, and so did all of our colleagues on the House Commerce Committee, and I think we did pretty well. And you mentioned light bulbs, which were a bipartisan initiative and passed on a bipartisan basis. Efficient light bulbs seems like a little thing, saves a huge amount of energy. We also did building standards and we did fuel efficiency and we did a number of other things.

I cannot vote here anymore, but I certainly support your initiative to help countries help themselves. It is a point we have all made about tough love for Ukraine. They have to take these steps, but we could give them tools that would help them take these steps. So I think others may want to comment, but I think this is a very good angle.

Finally, I said something—I am not sure you were here—about using our asymmetric strength against Russia. Our asymmetric strength is our economy. Our asymmetric strength is some of our good ideas like these. And the aid we give Ukraine could help with these ideas. And that would go a lot further than some of the other ideas that are more kinetic.

Senator MARKEY. May I ask each one of the witnesses—just very briefly. I do not have a lot of time—on this question of energy efficiency, natural gas? We have to help them with the reverse flow and other issues. Do you all agree this is an area we should really zero in on, and that will make the bigger long-term difference than any change in the LNG marketplace?

Ambassador PIFER. Certainly energy efficiency in Ukraine and helping Ukraine produce its own natural gas is a big thing. I think we actually may be moving in that direction. In 2012, the price that Ukrainian households paid for their heating gas was one-sixth the price that Ukraine was paying to import that. By raising the prices, they are going to introduce a huge incentive for all of those households to close the windows.

Senator MARKEY. Ambassador Jeffrey.

Ambassador JEFFREY. Absolutely, as two major components, along with others, and I would include us exporting LNG and encouraging Europe to get it from other sources as well.

Senator MARKEY. Even if it does increase electricity rates in the United States.

Ambassador JEFFREY. For reasons that go well beyond the Ukrainian problem.

Senator MARKEY. Congressman.

Ambassador GREEN. Senator, IRI does not take a position on energy legislation nor sanctions legislation. I will say that we believe in a comprehensive approach. So it is almost all of the above in terms of building capacity in Ukraine.

Mr. WOLLACK. With regard to technical expertise, however, the Ukrainian Government welcomes—on energy diversification and a host of all the reform issues, they welcome technical expertise in a major way as they go forward.

Senator MARKEY. I think that we really do have a huge opportunity here, and the more we learn about this country, the more we can see that it can be transformed in the blink of an eye. They could increase their energy efficiency by 10 percent in 2 years. They could increase their energy efficiency by 50 percent in 5 years. We have to use every bit of leverage that we have in order to help them accomplish that goal. That is what is going to keep Gazprom up at night with nightmares. That is why China looms larger in their life because they are going to see a market shrinking dramatically, and their geopolitical leverage as well, because that is what it is really all about.

Whether you talk about Syria or Iraq or Libya, unfortunately, oil underlies a lot of each one of those regions, and here we really get a chance to do something for them that makes them self-sustaining. And my hope is that we can talk about this issue on a bipartisan basis in the committee and get right at the heart of their weakness, get right at the heart of what this whole story is about, which is their necessity today of importing natural gas. But it is something that we can really change dramatically, and have Ukraine say to Russia, we do not need your natural gas any more than we need your soldiers. And that is a statement they should be able to make in the very near future if we help them to construct a plan and if we give them the help they need in order to be successful.

Thank you, Mr. Chairman.

The CHAIRMAN. Thank you. Senator Markey may be the newest member of the committee, but he is front and center on energy policy and global affairs. And we appreciate his expertise on the committee.

Two final questions. Ambassador Green, you have talked about this several times in your answers, and I would like to hear some other views as well. In Ukraine, yes, but in all of Eastern Europe the saturation the Russians have created with their broadcasting into the region, of course, is not open-ended broadcasting in terms of views. It is very much directed by the state.

What more should we really be doing with Voice of America and Radio Free Europe to quickly increase our level of engagement in this region, so that in addition to a domestically-created series of social networking platforms, there are additional opportunities for multiple voices to be heard?

Ambassador GREEN. Senator, I would argue that we should boost those programs, boost them into the regions, but we should also take a look at the social media platforms. There are ways that we can help to create anchors outside of the region such that it makes it harder for mischief. It makes it harder for the Russians to come in and shut them down. So it is helping to provide the technical expertise to foster the development of social media platforms that are indigenous in the region, but also taking steps to help reinforce and protect them from hostile moves such as we saw in eastern Ukraine.

The CHAIRMAN. Anyone else have thoughts?

Mr. WOLLACK. I would say we can also work with the Poles and others in Eastern Europe. So this is not just something the United States is doing. I think we have a lot of friends in the region in which we can enhance their capacity for broadcast and communications in Ukraine and also bolster the Ukrainian capacity in this regard as well.

The CHAIRMAN. Jane.

Ms. HARMAN. Well, just to reinforce Mark Green's earlier comments about social media, I think there is a huge voice in Ukraine that knows how to speak for itself. It just needs resources.

The CHAIRMAN. One final question, which I think is really an important one, but one which, in the focus of Ukraine, we have not talked about, and that is the nuclear nonproliferation implications of what has happened in Ukraine. Ukraine voluntarily surrendered their nuclear weapons that they inherited from the former Soviet Union, in exchange for a commitment by Russia, as well as the United Kingdom and the United States, to respect Ukraine's territorial integrity.

Are there implications for global nonproliferation regimes with the loss of Crimea and the threat to eastern Ukraine? Is there a conclusion that if Ukraine had retained these nuclear weapons, the loss of Crimea would not have happened and therefore possession of nuclear weapons is the only guarantee of territorial integrity when threatened by another nuclear power such as the Russians? I am concerned that at some point some are going to rivet their attention to that. In some of my travels, I have heard a little bit of that from other countries. I would like to hear if anybody has any perspectives on that.

Ambassador PIFER. Mr. Chairman, actually I helped negotiate the 1994 Budapest Memorandum of Security Assurances, which was part of the agreement by which Ukraine gave up its nuclear weapons.

And I think one of the tragedies of what the Russians have done with their assault and the annexation of Crimea and in their continued action in eastern Ukraine, which is violating the commitments they made in that document to respect Ukraine's territorial integrity, sovereignty, not to use force against Ukraine, is that they have now devalued the idea of security assurances which could have been a tool in other proliferation cases. For example, it might have been part of the solution on Iran or North Korea at some point. And so one of the reasons why I think it is now incumbent on the United States and Britain, who cosigned the Budapest Memorandum—one of the reasons why we should be doing things to support Ukraine but also to penalize Russia is to make clear that there are, in fact, consequences for violating those sorts of commitments. But the Russians have done grievous damage to the ability of security assurances of the Budapest Memorandum kind to be part of a solution in future proliferation cases.

Ambassador JEFFREY. I agree with Steve.

But from the standpoint of the Middle East where I spent much of my time and effort in the past and now, what is important is what happens in the days, weeks, months, years ahead. If the Russian action is punished at an ever greater degree of power by the international community, if Crimea is not acknowledged as basically Russian, the way we just forgot about South Ossetia, if we can show that there are military and other actions that, first of all, will preserve the bulk of Ukraine will make it a vibrant part of the Western community in the future, then I think countries will say, yes, led by the United States, the West stood up to that aggression. And there is an international alternative to us developing not just weapons of mass destruction but large armies and little 1914 kind of local coalitions and other things that, taken together, are going to undercut this global order. So we have got a lot of work ahead of us to ensure not just for the sake of Ukraine, but for the sake of nonproliferation and the overall international order that, just to quote an earlier American President, ''this shall not stand.''

The CHAIRMAN. Well, this has been a very insightful panel. We appreciate you all sharing your time, as well as your expertise and your insights.

This record will remain open until the close of business on Friday.

And with the gratitude of the committee, this hearing is adjourned.

[Whereupon, at 12:10 p.m., the hearing was adjourned.]

ADDITIONAL MATERIAL SUBMITTED FOR THE RECORD

PREPARED STATEMENT OF THE NDI ELECTION OBSERVER DELEGATION TO UKRAINE'S 2014 PRESIDENTIAL ELECTION SUBMITTED BY KENNETH WOLLACK

This preliminary statement is offered by the National Democratic Institute (NDI) election observer delegation to Ukraine's May 25, 2014, Presidential election. Former Secretary of State Madeleine Albright, NDI's chairman, and Ana Palacio, former Foreign Minister of Spain, cochaired the delegation. Other members of the delegation's leadership group included former U.S. Senator Edward ''Ted'' Kaufman of Delaware; former U.S. Representative Jane Harman of California, director, president and CEO of the Wilson Center; and Matyas Eorsi, former member of Parliament from Hungary and former member of the Parliamentary Assembly of the Council of Europe.

This preliminary statement is offered as votes are being tabulated and any electoral complaints that may be lodged are yet to be processed. NDI therefore does not seek to offer its final analysis of the election, and it recognizes that ultimately the people of Ukraine will determine the meaning of the election as they exercise their sovereignty. NDI's mission operated in conformance with the Declaration of Principles for International Election Observation and Ukrainian law, and it cooperated with nonpartisan citizen election monitors and other international observer missions that endorse the Declaration.

The delegation wishes to express its appreciation to the United States Agency for International Development (USAID), which has funded the work of this delegation and, along with the National Endowment for Democracy (NED) and the Swedish International Development Cooperation Agency (SIDA), has supported NDI democracy assistance programs in Ukraine.

SUMMARY

Ukrainians have achieved a democratic milestone. By turning out to vote yesterday across the vast majority of the country, Ukrainians did more than elect a new President. They showed the world their commitment to sovereignty, unity, and democracy. Their votes expressed the clear aspiration that these principles be valued over geopolitical strategy or leaders' personal enrichment. Despite constraints, Ukraine's electoral administrators, campaigns, government authorities, election monitors and voters showed courage and resolve in fulfilling their responsibilities in compliance with Ukraine's laws and international democratic election standards. The candidates deserve commendation for their constructive responses to the results.

The Russian occupation of Crimea prevented any voting in that region. Armed groups interfered with electoral preparations and voting in large parts of the Donetsk and Luhansk oblasts—two of five eastern provinces. The disenfranchisement of voters in these places represents a serious violation of rights. At the same time, it does not negate the legitimacy of the overall election or the mandate it provides. A democratic election process should not be held hostage to foreign occupation or illegal actions by armed separatists seeking to disrupt the democratic process.

In those places where voting took place, the elections were generally well run and proceeded without major incidents. Large numbers of domestic and international observers mobilized across all of Ukraine to safeguard the integrity of the process. In observing elections in more than 60 countries since 1986, including previous polls in Ukraine, rarely has NDI heard such positive commentary from political contestants and monitors.

This democratic election can begin a process to reinforce public confidence in the country's political institutions. The task ahead for the new President, as well as other political and government leaders, will be to pursue open and consultative governing practices that incorporate the interests of Ukrainians from all regions of the country. The leaders must communicate effectively the prospect of short-term sacrifices, and deliver on the longer term expectations of the Euromaidan movement.

The task is great. These expectations include:

• An accountable government;
• Political institutions that channel dissent, facilitate debate, and respond effectively to citizens' concerns;
• Transparency and integrity in all aspects of public life;
• An open and fair judicial process;
• An electoral system that encourages new faces and ideas; and
• A legislative process that is based on consultation and open debate.

These are ideals to which even established democracies aspire, but Ukraine has reached a moment in history where that path is once again open to it. Some meaningful reforms have already been undertaken; many more are needed for Ukraine to reach its democratic potential.

I. POLITICAL CONTEXT

This was the most important election in Ukraine's independent history. It came at a critical moment following a groundswell of citizen political engagement prompted by the Euromaidan movement and amid challenges to the country's sovereignty and territorial integrity.

The Euromaidan demonstrations that began in November 2013 fundamentally altered the political dynamics in Ukraine. They highlighted Ukrainians' demands for change, including more transparent, accountable, and uncorrupted political practices as well as respect for basic civil and political rights. Euromaidan was sparked by anger over the government's abrupt refusal to sign the EU-Ukraine Association Agreement, but it was sustained for three months by a more basic demand for dignity and respect from government. Euromaidan drew participants from across the country and spawned similar demonstrations in cities in all regions, reflecting widespread consensus on these issues. Public opinion research by several respected sources through April and May also demonstrates that Ukrainians across regions share a desire for national unity, more responsive governance and greater public integrity.

Tragically, the Euromaidan demonstrations culminated in the deaths of more than 100 Ukrainians and injuries to many more. Other deaths in the East and South, including those in a fire in Odessa, present the need for a concerted reconciliation process.

The country is facing serious challenges: an economic crisis; an inherited deficit of confidence in political institutions; internal differences of opinion about the country's future course; and most significantly, occupation of territory and, in other regions, armed insurrections aimed at disrupting political processes. An inclusive public mandate will help the government address these challenges.

In the aftermath of the May 25 vote, it is hoped that the national dialogue on ensuring rights and representation for all Ukrainians will accelerate and deepen. The best legacy of Euromaidan would be a politically active and engaged citizenry combined with responsive and accountable institutions that together preclude the need for future Maidans. It will take concerted efforts from all citizens of the country to address the many economic, political, and security challenges facing Ukraine in the days and months ahead.

The international community has a critical responsibility to be engaged over the long term with assistance—financial, diplomatic, and technical. This support must be set in the context of respect for territorial integrity, promotion of fundamental rights, and a commitment to the country's democratic and economic development. Ukrainians have said that they welcome technical assistance, which would be integrated into their reform efforts.

II. ELECTION DAY

Three types of elections were held on May 25: the Presidential vote; one single-mandate parliamentary race; and a series of local polls (more than 40 mayors, including Kiev, 27 settlement executives, 200 village executives, plus two city councils, including Kiev, and three village councils).

In 23 of Ukraine's 27 administrative units (24 oblasts, the republic of Crimea, and the cities of Kiev and Sevastopol), the elections were generally well run and proceeded without major incidents. Overall turnout is now estimated at 60 percent. By contrast, in Crimea, Donetsk, and Luhansk, representing just under 20 percent of the electorate, most voters were denied the opportunity to exercise their franchise.

In most of the country, voting proceeded unhindered. The pre-election period and Presidential election were virtually free of formal candidate complaints. Political party representatives comprising the polling station commissions (PECs) cooperated with each other to facilitate voting and address issues, while large numbers of nonpartisan citizen observers and party poll watchers witnessed the procedures, including many women among their ranks. Across the country, voters often stood in long lines waiting patiently to cast their votes.

Isolated problems were significant in some places, including, for example, Molotov cocktails thrown at three PECs the night before the elections in the southern city of Kherson, though all opened on time for voting, and in Mykolaiv, also in the South, bomb threats briefly closed at least seven PECs, though voting resumed in each of them. The delegation did observe incidents of overcrowding at polling sites (particularly in Kiev, Lviv, and Sumy), police presence inside polling stations (in Zaporizhia), and late arrival of mobile ballot boxes (Odessa). Also, most polling places were not easily accessible by voters with disabilities. There were concerns prior to the elections about a possible lack of quorums of polling site officials, problems related to large-scale substitutions of those officials immediately prior to the elections, and the inability of security forces to respond to disruptions. These concerns, however, were not realized.

No polling took place in Crimea due to the Russian occupation. Crimea is home to 1.5 million registered voters, representing 5 percent of the Ukrainian electorate. The Central Election Commission (CEC) reported that approximately 6,000 Crimean residents registered to vote in other parts of the country, which was the only procedure available to them.

In Donetsk and Luhansk, illegal actions by armed groups—including seizures of government buildings and electoral facilities, abductions and killings of journalists and widespread intimidation—aimed to derail the elections. Even in the face of such violations of people's fundamental rights, electoral officials opened nearly 20 percent of polling stations in those two oblasts. International and nonpartisan Ukrainian election observers witnessed their brave and determined efforts by these officials.

The delegation deeply regrets any violations of voters' rights to exercise their franchise, including those which occurred in Crimea, Donetsk, and Luhansk. Universal and equal suffrage for eligible citizens is fundamental to democratic elections. However, these three cases should not negate the fact that the vast majority of the electorate—well more than 80 percent—had the opportunity to cast their ballots for the candidate of their choice.

Also, it is important to note the source of voter disenfranchisement. In most countries where NDI has observed disenfranchisement, it has been caused by authorities or political contestants interfering with the process for electoral advantage. In Crimea, Donetsk, and Luhansk, the responsibility lies with the foreign forces occupying

Ukrainian territory and armed groups seeking to derail the electoral process, despite good faith efforts of election officials. Such disenfranchisement cannot be allowed to negate the legitimacy of elections or the mandate they provide. Unfortunately, disenfranchisement has occurred in parts of Afghanistan, Pakistan, and Georgia in recent elections due to terrorism by nonstate actors or foreign occupation. Nevertheless, those actions did not delegitimize those elections.

Election Observation

Large numbers of nonpartisan citizen election observers mobilized across all of Ukraine to safeguard the integrity of the election process and promote public confidence. The Civic Network Opora and the Committee of Voters of Ukraine (CVU) each mobilized approximately 150 long-term monitors and issued reports leading to the elections; each group fielded approximately 2,000 election-day observers in all regions. Opora also mounted systematic election-day observation of the voting, counting and tabulation processes through deploying monitors to a representative statistical sample of polling stations that allowed it to issue reports on the quality of the opening of polls, turnout and critical aspects of the processes.

These observers had full access to the processes under the law, the authority to lodge official electoral complaints and witness entry of results at the district election commissions (DECs) into the CEC's computerized results tabulation system. This level of transparency added to confidence in election-day procedures. Ukrainian citizen observers courageously deployed to all parts of the country except Crimea. At times they faced difficult circumstances.

The OSCE's Office for Democratic Institutions and Human Rights (OSCE/ODIHR) was responsible for organizing approximately 1,000 election-day observers, including 100 long-term observers (LTOs) who were in place across across the country beginning on March 27, except in Crimea. This effort was joined by the OSCE Parliamentary Assembly, the Parliamentary Assembly of the Council of Europe (PACE) and other bodies. The European Network of Election Monitoring Organizations (ENEMO) deployed 50 LTOs and 300 additional election-day observers. The International Republican Institute (IRI) also observed the election. These observer missions, along with NDI, cooperated in their observation efforts. Each of these missions reported that they received cooperation from election authorities at all levels.

III. ELECTORAL FRAMEWORK AND PREELECTION ENVIRONMENT

The pre-election period was compressed due to the constitutional requirement to hold elections within 90 days of a President being unable to fulfill the duties of the office. Nonetheless, NDI has rarely heard such positive commentary on the election process as it has from contestants and observers in these elections. This includes the Institute's monitoring of elections in more than 60 countries since 1986, including previous polls in Ukraine. Traditional violations, such as misuse of state resources for electoral advantage, vote buying and intimidation were not raised as issues by the candidates, observers or election officials, though they were prominent in several past Ukrainian elections.

Electoral Framework and Administration

March 2014 amendments to the Presidential election law brought the framework into compliance with international standards and responded to many previous recommendations from domestic and international observers. The CEC as well as most district and precinct commissions performed professionally and, in some cases, with notable courage. Election commissioners and precinct premises were targeted with threats and violence in Donetsk and Luhansk. Those who fulfilled their responsibilities in the face of significant security risks in some parts of the country deserve particular commendation.

Campaigns and Candidates

The 21 Presidential candidates on the ballot represented a broad range of political perspectives and parties, including the former ruling party. Campaigning was muted compared to previous Presidential elections, due to events in parts of the east, but the candidates and their teams were able to communicate with voters freely in most parts of the country. Campaign messages overwhelmingly focused on peace, stability, and Ukrainian unity. More traditional "pocketbook" issues like jobs, education and healthcare were not central to the campaigns. Violence and instability prevented normal campaigning in Donetsk and Luhansk.

Media Environment

In most of the country, media freedoms were generally respected. Journalists were able to operate without interference and voters had access to multiple media perspectives, although coverage of the campaign was downplayed in favor of events in the south and east. There were some reports of unattributed paid advertising and socalled "black PR," and some media outlets were seen to favor particular candidates.

In Crimea, Donetsk and Luhansk, however, media freedoms came under attack. Journalists faced censorship, harassment, violence, and kidnapping. On the eve of the election, a journalist was murdered. In addition, a pro-Russia disinformation campaign aimed at discrediting the Ukrainian Government and its supporters permeated the pre-election environment.

Women's Participation

Women represent 54 percent of the Ukrainian population, but they are underrepresented in politics as leaders. Only two Presidential candidates were women. The delegation did not see strong evidence that Presidential or local government campaigns systematically promoted women as candidates or campaigners, nor systematically targeted support from women voters.

Campaign Financing

The corrosive role of money in politics is a major area of concern that has not yet been adequately addressed in legislation or practice. The amendments to the Presidential election law do little to control or bring transparency to campaign finances. Some Presidential candidates voluntarily disclosed on their Web sites sources and amounts of donations and expenditures. These are welcome steps, but before any future elections, consideration should be given to regulatory and legislative frameworks that would address these longstanding concerns.

IV. THE DELEGATION AND ITS WORK

The NDI delegation's coleaders, Albright and Palacio, symbolize the importance of a trans-Atlantic commitment to a democratic Ukraine. The delegation arrived in Kiev on May 21 and held meetings with national political leaders, Presidential candidates, election officials, senior government officials, representatives of nongovernmental organizations, the media and the diplomatic community. On May 24–25, observers deployed in teams to 11 regions across Ukraine, including Kiev, where they met with regional and local government representatives, election administrators, and political and civic leaders. On election day, the NDI teams observed voting and counting processes in polling stations across the country.

In addition to Albright, Palacio, Harman, Kaufman, and Eorsi, members of the delegation included:

- Brian Atwood, former administrator of the U.S. Agency for International Development (USAID) and former president of NDI;
- Hattie Babbitt, former U.S. Ambassador to the Organization of American States, former deputy administrator of USAID and a member of the NDI Board;
- Richard Blum, chairman and president of Blum Capital Partners and a member of the NDI Board;
- Patrick Griffin, former assistant to the president and director for legislative affairs under President Clinton and member of the NDI Board;
- Rick Inderfurth, former assistant secretary of state for South Asian affairs and former U.S. representative for special political affairs at the U.N.;
- Kurt MacLeod, vice president for Asia and Eurasia at Pact;
- Sarah Mendelson, former deputy assistant administrator at USAID;
- Sharon Nazarian, president of the Y&S Nazarian Family Foundation;
- James O'Brien, vice chair of the Albright Stonebridge Group;
- Stephen Sestanovich, former U.S. Ambassador at Large for the former Soviet Union and a professor of international diplomacy at Columbia University;
- William Taylor, former U.S. Ambassador to Ukraine and vice president for the Middle East and Africa at the U.S. Institute of Peace;
- Kenneth Wollack, president of NDI;
- Pat Merloe, director of electoral programs at NDI;
- Ermek Adylbekov, program manager in NDI's Kyrgyzstan office;
- Catherine Cecil, NDI's resident director in Ukraine;
- Kathy Gest, director of public affairs at NDI;
- Laura Jewett, NDI's regional director for Eurasia;
- Daniel Mitov, NDI's resident representative in Brussels and former executive director of the Democracy Foundation in Bulgaria;
- Teona Kupunia, senior program officer in NDI's Georgia office;
- Tinatin Museridze, senior administrative and financial manager in NDI's Georgia office;
- Gegham Sargsyanm NDI's resident country director in Armenia;

- Andrei Strah, a consultant to NDI in Moldova; and
- Aida Suyundueva, formerly of NDI's offices in Kyrgyzstan and Azerbaijan.

The mission builds on the ongoing observations of NDI's long-term analysts, who have worked with the Institute's Kiev-based staff since April, and the findings of NDI's April 7–11 pre-election assessment mission. Ted Kaufman and Matyas Eorsi, members of this delegation, also participated in the pre-election assessment. NDI also issued a May 9 statement on separatist referendums and a second pre-election statement on May 19. NDI's 38 observers visited polling stations in districts across Ukraine. In addition to its international observation activities, NDI supported the election monitoring efforts of Opora and ENEMO.

NDI is a nonprofit, nonpartisan organization working to support and strengthen democratic institutions worldwide through citizen participation, openness and accountability in government. NDI has monitored 340 elections and organized more than 150 international election observer missions in 63 countries, including four pre-election and election day assessments in Ukraine.